1971

ay be l

SEX AND CHRISTIAN FREEDOM

An Enquiry

Sex and Christian Freedom

AN ENQUIRY

LEONARD HODGSON

THE SEABURY PRESS
NEW YORK

CONTENTS

PREFACE

FOR MORE THAN half a century I have been professionally a theologian. But essentially I am a philosopher in the socratic sense of being unable to avoid questioning whatever I find other people taking for granted. This applies equally to the exponents of new ideas and to the champions of old. My professional studies are thus the work of a socratic philosopher doing theology. I have called this book 'An Enquiry' because, again like Socrates, to many of the questions I not only don't know the answers, but I know that I don't know them.

I make no apology for the mingling of autobiography with argument. In all argument what each party is actually saying is: 'This is how I see it. Can't you see it too?' How can one better explain how he sees anything than by trying to show how in his own experience he has been brought to his point of view?

A friend who has read the typescript has warned me that my first chapter may only be of interest to older readers, and that in chapters 2 and 3 I am attempting to combine two books, one about the Bible and the other about sex ethics. My reply is that the aim of the book is to bring the two together. If I published them separately those who would read the one would probably not read the other, and all would miss the point. Moreover, the book is about *Christian* sex ethics. Some who read only the last chapter (especially among older readers) might be inclined to dismiss it with the *cliché* that this is just the so-called new morality which is nothing but a new name for the old immorality. Therefore it was necessary to secure the ground for chapter 6 by showing how it is based on biblical foundations, as well as on the understanding of ethics described in chapter 1.

I can never adequately express what I owe to the many friends who have helped me in discussing questions raised in this enquiry. Gratitude is especially due to my colleagues at William Temple College. Chapter by chapter most of them have read the first drafts as they came off the typewriter. They have by no means always agreed with me, but subsequent revisions have greatly profited from their criticisms, comments and suggestions. For the version here finally printed I am myself alone responsible.

Two books have appeared too late for me to take note of them while writing: The British Council of Churches' Working Party Report on *Sex and Morality* and R. F. Hettlinger's *Living with Sex: The Student's Dilemma*. Both are now published in England by the SCM Press. I welcome them both as enriching my own somewhat narrow academic experience of life from their fuller experience of pastoral ministry. But if we are to be discussing Christian sex ethics, then it seems to me that their conclusions need to be more firmly grounded in biblical and theological foundations than they have set themselves to provide. I shall be content if my professional studies have enabled me to show my fellow clergy that in our counselling work we can talk twentieth-century common sense without being disloyal to our ordination vows.

L. H.

I

ETHICAL ABSOLUTES AND RELATIVES

I

I WAS IN my twelfth year when Queen Victoria died. I had been born into a churchgoing family and was brought up in the Christian faith by which (as I said at the end of my Gifford Lectures) I have tried to live and in which I hope to die. That was a bygone world, and while the faith in which I hope to die is essentially the same as that into which I was born, the form in which I hold it now is in many ways different from that which I took for granted at the opening of the twentieth century. In various books I have told the tale of the transformation with regard to Bible study and Christian doctrine. I want now to consider its bearing on some of our present-day questions in the field of morals.

In my youth I was given to understand that Christian moral standards had been revealed by God and were of absolute, universal and eternal validity. In the Catechism of the Church of England they were summed up in the exposition of the Ten Commandments as the Duties to God and neighbour. But biblical authority was also claimed for more detailed application of these general statements. Thus it was held that by the teaching of Christ and St Paul 'to keep my body in temperance, soberness and chastity' ruled out all pre-marital or extramarital sexual intercourse and divorce. It might be thought that 'not to covet nor desire other men's goods', 'to be true and just in all my doings', and 'to keep my tongue from lying' would have been found irreconcilable with many accepted practices in business and politics. But Christianity was generally held to be concerned with the morals of individuals, with the question of their salvation out of this sinful world for eternal bliss in heaven. Pious heads might be shaken over the wickedness of the world; tender consciences might be troubled by inability to avoid compromise. The troubling was due to the conviction that we knew the absolute, universal and eternal rules by which we ought to be living. Right was right and wrong was wrong and we knew which was which.

I cannot remember at what age I first met the challenge to this comfortable sense of assurance. But I do remember that it came as a distinct shock. It took the form of pointing out how different were the moral codes taken for granted with equal assurance by different groups of men and women in different ages and different places in the world's history. The words 'ethical' and 'moral' did not refer to any divinely revealed absolute standards; their derivation from Greek and Latin showed that they meant conformity to the accepted custom of this or that community.

The immediate reaction was to swing over to the opposite pole, to conclude that since all moral judgments are relative to the presuppositions accepted by different communities, there are none which have absolutely binding authority. All questions of right or wrong conduct are in the melting pot. Ethics is a field in which there are no absolutes.

To cut a long story short, I have now come to see that there are two opposite errors to be avoided. The fact that our ethical standards are in the melting pot does not mean that this is a field in which there are no absolutes. It means that our knowledge of them is imperfect. We are tempted on the one hand to think that we know what they are and that all we have to do is to assert them; when we find that rules we have taken to be universally binding are questioned by men of equal good will and our ideas are shown to be conditioned by the tradition in which we have been brought up, we are tempted to despair of ever again being able to feel solid ground under our feet.

Because of the tradition in which we have been brought up we Christians are especially liable to the former of these temptations. Too many attempted replies to present-day questioning of Christian ethical standards are still based on this assumption. What I now wish to maintain is that the right way to avoid falling into the second of these temptations is to hold that in ethics, as in other fields of learning, God is leading us on to share more fully in his knowledge of what our standards should be. At each stage in human history we have to be content to try to live by what we have so far come to see, while we look to him to lead us further on into better and fuller understanding.

What I have to say is the application to ethics of the way of thinking about revelation which in other respects I have worked out elsewhere, notably in my Gifford Lectures.[1] A brief summary is necessary to prepare for what follows.

The history of human thought is the history of man learning to know the nature of the universe and of himself within it. This comes by observation of what exists and happens and by reflection upon it. All such observation and reflection is made by men and women from the point of view of particular times and places, their minds conditioned by the traditions in which they have grown up. Their thoughts and their statements are coloured by their presuppositions, and if there is to be any advance in knowledge it will come by successive ages learning to observe more accurately and intelligently, so that in studying the work of their predecessors genuine insights can be distinguished from miscolourings due to particular presuppositions or personal idiosyncrasies. Human knowledge grows through a continuing tension in which minds formed by inherited traditions seek to assimilate new evidence, asking

[1] *For Faith and Freedom* (Oxford, Vol. I, 1956; Vol. II, 1957).

what revision of existing categories of thought may be necessary if the present age is to make its contribution to man's
understanding of himself and his world.

To the Christian believer this is all part of divine revelation. God reveals himself in his activity and by inspiring men
to see things and events as revelatory. In his creative activity
he makes himself known to us through the arts and the
sciences; in his redemptive activity through a certain series of
events in history, still continuing today, to which the Bible
bears witness; in his inspiring activity through all who
honestly seek to increase man's knowledge of truth and to
make good use of the forces of nature. One facet of the
mystery of evil is the fact that in the pursuit of truth we have
to struggle with error. We can only see things with the eyes of
our own age and culture, and the inherited presuppositions
which colour our outlook are a mixture of insights and dis-
tortions. In studying the history of human thought we are
studying the human end, the receiving end, of the activity of
God the Holy Spirit as he enables men to discount successive
layers of presuppositions which colour, and often miscolour,
the way they see the truth.

Meanwhile God is eternal. He knows the truth of all things,
in whole and in detail. What light we can get on the dark
mystery of evil comes from our belief that he wills to create
beings who are not automata but genuine persons who are to
reach their full manhood by growth in freedom. Thus all our
knowledge is relative in the sense of being the best that we can
see from our point of view in space and time. But our views
are relative not only to what has been seen in the past and to
what some of our contemporaries may see differently; they
are also relative to the full knowledge towards which we are
making progress, which alone can rightly be called knowledge.
In so far as we have any grasp of truth it is a glimpse of some
facet of that full truth, such approximation to it as is open to
us here and now.

This is what makes it possible for some of our relative judgments to have, as it were, a touch of absoluteness. If growth in knowledge of truth is one of the ways in which God is leading mankind to the fulfilment of his creative purpose for us, we may expect that some of the lessons we learn will give us firm ground from which to set out on further advance. There can be no progress if every generation has to go back and start afresh from square one. In the history of our religion the standard of honesty enjoined in Psalm 15 is an advance on that approved in the stories about Jacob. The slavery taken for granted in New Testament times becomes irreconcilable with the Christian conscience. There is no going back on the fact that those of us who are not pacifists have an uneasy conscience on the subject of war. The church is in process of revising its thought about so-called birth control or family planning.

We have to combine holding fast to the truth we have already learned with an open-minded expectation that we still have more to learn, and that the learning of it may involve the revision of some of our cherished notions.

In the seventeenth century the English poet Richard Lovelace wrote the well-known lines:

> I could not love thee, dear, so much
> Loved I not honour more.

In this England of the twentieth century it is good to be reminded that three hundred years ago we had got so far as to realize that for human beings the stirrings of the mating urge have to be woven into the fabric of a life in which other considerations may have to be given priority. What are those other considerations? How can we best reconcile the claims of the absolute and the relative in the formulation of a Christian sex ethic for today? Because we are still in process of learning what God has to teach us, we can have no exposition which is not also a matter of enquiry.

II

As a first step in this enquiry we must examine some of the factors which produce the element of relativity in our ethical judgments.

1. The most important of these is the fact that we are in process of being created into persons as individualized centres of responsible activity, each through the experience of his life in some particular place and time in the world's history. The familiar controversy between utilitarians and deontologists often seems to me to be carried on in a way which pays too little attention to this:

According to utilitarianism, an act is good or right if it pro-motes human welfare; its moral quality is to be discovered by an examination of its consequences. Thus the reason why we ought to keep our word is that any social life worth living is impossible on a basis of untrustworthiness. According to the moral law school, an act is right or good if it is done in obedi-ence to an eternal moral law. The reason why we ought to keep our word is that to break it is 'wrong in itself', whatever the consequences.[2]

This way of describing the dispute implies that it is possible to isolate acts and circumstances and consider each on its own with a view to drawing up a list of what acts are right and what wrong, what are worthy of praise and what deserve blame. But the more I think about it, the more I become un-able to make this disjunction. I can give no meaning to the word 'act' other than 'response to a situation'. Thus the cir-cumstances go to the making of the act what it is. Abstracted from them it has no character worth mentioning. 'Drinking' becomes simply pouring liquid down a throat. It may be con-stituted a morally significant act by such circumstances as the alcoholic content, whether it be the first, second, third or further glass, and the comparative strength of the drinker's

[2] L. Hodgson, *The Doctrine of the Atonement* (London, 1951), p. 19.

head. Circumstances decide whether a killing is murder or justifiable homicide.

It is possible to draw up lists of morally graded acts, to say, for example, that murder, theft, adultery, 'evil speaking, lying and slandering' are bad. But such a list must always be subject to the qualification that each instance has to be judged in relation to the circumstances which have made the act what it was.

2. The ideal response would be that which objectively is the right act in the circumstances and is done from the right motive. Sometimes we do the right thing from the wrong motive; sometimes the wrong thing from the right motive. When making ethical judgments it is essential to clear thinking to distinguish whether what we say refers to the objective rightness or wrongness of what is done or to the agent's motive.

3. If every act is a response to a situation, an understanding of the situation is necessary for an estimate of its moral value. We live in what Christian theologians call a 'fallen world', in other words, a world in which good and evil are so interwoven as to produce situations in which none of the courses open to us is free from evil. The stock illustration of this in the textbooks is the case in which we have to choose between telling a lie and breaking a confidence. On this Nicolai Hartmann has well said:

It is not the values as such in their pure ideality which are in conflict; between the claim of truthfulness as such and the duty of the soldier or friend there exists no antinomy at all. The conflict arises from the structure of the situation. This makes it impossible to satisfy both at the same time. But if from this one should think to make out a universal justification of the necessary lie, one would err as much as if one were to attempt a universal justification for violating one's duty to one's country or the duty of keeping one's promise.

Nevertheless a man who is in such a situation cannot avoid making a decision. Every attempt to remain neutral only makes the difficulty worse, in that he violates both values; the attempt not to commit oneself is at bottom moral cowardice.[3]

This earth is not heaven, and quite often the doing of God's will in it cannot be done in the same way as it could be done in heaven. Without an understanding of the situation it is impossible to judge the rightness or wrongness of the response.

Both the exponents and the critics of so-called 'situational ethics' tend to underestimate the importance of the time factor in God's providential ordering of his creation.[4] They overlook the fact that human judgments can only be made from the point of view of men of their own age. They must be seen in the context of the ongoing ethical education of men by God. Dr Ramsey's way of drawing the contrast between 'act-ethics' and 'rule-ethics' obscures the fact that the claim of a situation to be treated as an exception may be due to its being one in which a morally courageous decision which runs counter to hitherto accepted rules will be the means through which God opens our eyes to see how rules need to be revised. Case law as well as statute law has a contribution to make to our growth in the knowledge of God's will.

As a matter of terminology I find it useful to make a distinction. I try to keep 'good' and 'evil' for what God has taught us to think intrinsically good or evil, what gives to 'some of our ethical judgments . . . a touch of absoluteness'. I keep 'right' and 'wrong' for the relative element, the response required by the situation which may or may not be good. 'When a man is faced by a choice of evils, the choice of the lesser evil may be called right but not good. What is wrong is always evil, but what is right is not always good.'[5]

4. Since all our knowledge is relative in the sense of being the best that we can see from our point of view in space and

[3] N. Hartmann, *Ethics* (E. Tr. S. Coit, London, 1932), Vol. II, p. 284.
[4] See e.g. Paul Lehmann, *Ethics in a Christian Context* (London, 1963); Joseph Fletcher, *Situation Ethics* (London, 1966); Paul Ramsey, *Deeds and Rules in Christian Ethics* (Edinburgh and London, 1965).
[5] Cp. *For Faith and Freedom*, Vol. I, p. 147.

time, both acts and motives must be judged in the light of their contemporary climate of thought. It would not be fair, for example, to condemn St Paul for having accepted the institution of slavery. If I am right in holding that God both has been and still is educating us in ethical understanding, this applies both to our historical studies of the past and to our attempts to understand the problems of the present and the future. Witness the testimony of the Rev. Jean Kotto, General Secretary of the Evangelical Church of Cameroun:

. . . the categorical refusal to admit polygamists as church members even if they have accepted Jesus Christ as Lord and Saviour and are begging to be accepted into the church. The big copper-magnate who exploits 40,000 underpaid, badly-housed labourers is a good church member. But the polygamist who remains faithful to his wives, all working peacefully together for the good of the family, is not allowed to join the church. His wives are also excluded, and even his children; the church refuses to baptize them at all—even later on in their lifetime—unless the man sends all his wives away except one. What is to happen to those wives who are sent away and to their children separated from the affection of the family in these rapidly changing societies? They can only become prostitutes and outcasts who are hostile to the church. And what happens to those polygamists who are refused admission to the church after giving them a taste for religion? They become Moslems. Africa is already betrothed to Islam. What are we doing to prevent this marriage taking place? The roots of polygamy in Africa go too deep to be destroyed by a general ruling which attempts to force people into monogamy. We complain about the secularization of society. But we do not complain about the narrowness and weakness of our own church regulations which try to force people instead of educating them. This is what Karl Barth says in his book on church dogma: 'While theological ethics definitely advocate monogamy and oppose polygamy, the purpose of this must be recognized, but on no account must brutal methods be employed. Cases certainly exist in which the immediate abolition of polygamy (that is, sending away all a polygamist's wives except one) is a cruel mistake, with no ethical justification.'[6]

⁶ *The Ecumenical Review* (October 1963), p. 74.

III

Taken together St Paul's acceptance of slavery and Jean Kotto's reflections on polygamy show how complex is the question of understanding what should be the Christian sex ethic at the present time.

For St Paul the time had not yet come for the inconsistency of slavery with the mind of Christ to be revealed. His understanding of the Christian ethic was conditioned by his belonging to his own age. It was coloured by presuppositions from some of which it needed to be delivered as God continued the education of his successors. Is it possible that in the traditional Christian ethic as handed down to us from his time there are also other inconsistent elements which have not yet been discovered and cast out, an infiltration of Christian thought, for example, by sex tabus of alien origin?

We have seen that from the ethical point of view an act is a response to a situation, and that circumstances go to the making of it the kind of act it is. Jean Kotto reminds us that among the circumstances to be taken into account an important part is played by the habits and customs of the prevailing civilization. Is it possible that, in this England of the second half of the twentieth century AD, the position of Christian monogamy is more like that in the Cameroun than we commonly like to admit?

These are the questions we have to ask, the enquiry which must precede any attempt at exposition.

For the second question we need the help of those whose fields of study are psychology and the social sciences. The first reminds us that we need their help at an early stage of our work. It is only too easy for us to think that we already know what is the Christian sex ethic, that all we have to do is to expound it, commend it, and call on our fellow men and women to try to live by it, quoting from psychologists and sociologists when they seem to agree with what we say and ignoring them when they do not. But this would be to ignore what we have learnt about the nature of God's method in revelation. A recollection of what it has meant elsewhere may throw light on its relevance in the field of morals.

An intelligent Christian who is asked today what he means by the doctrine of creation will state it in a form very different from that which would have been presented by his predecessor of a hundred-and-fifty years ago. This transformation has come about through the fact that from various lines of scientific research we have learnt more of the actual history of how the universe has come into its present state than was known before.[7] It may be that as we have had to learn from the physical and biological sciences how to revise our understanding of God's creative activity, so now he is calling on us to learn from the sciences which study human behaviour how we may enter into a fuller understanding of his will for the ordering of our lives.

But first we must pause to consider the theological question of how we think of God himself.

[7] Cp. *For Faith and Freedom*, Vol. I, pp. 121ff.

2

HOW DO WE THINK OF GOD?

I

LONG EXPERIENCE HAS taught me that the fundamental
question underlying every theological statement is, What are
its implications for belief about God? Is it consistent with
thinking about God as the God revealed to us in Jesus Christ?
Any attempt, therefore, to discuss a Christian sex ethic must
begin by asking what idea of God it will have to imply.

Science and religion both had their origin in primitive
attempts to get in touch with whatever forces control the
course of nature and the fortunes of men. Our science is the
lineal descendant of the magic which treated them as imper-
sonal forces to be controlled by discovering the appropriate
formula or ritual practice. Our religion is the development of
attempts to approach them as personal deities or spirits, to gain
the favour of those disposed to be beneficent, to placate or pro-
pitiate those who were not. This development can be studied
in the various religions of mankind. Our present concern with
it is in the history of Hebrew and Christian thought, in which
we must pay special attention to the insights of the prophets
in the Old Testament and the teaching of Jesus Christ in the
New.

I have described the history of human thought as a process
in which in every age men's minds are conditioned by the outlook of their place and time.[1] As we study the work of our
predecessors we seek to sift the ore of their genuine and en-

[1] See above, p. 11.

during insights from the expendable alloy due to their presuppositions. Our historical studies aim at discovering the provenance of documents and the outlook of their authors. Then we have to ask what the truth must have been and be if men with that outlook saw it like that. In what follows I am not attempting to give an exegetical account of what was in the minds of the Hebrew prophets but to draw out the implications for us of their teaching about God. In this there are three features on which I want to dwell.

1. God is thought of as the one and only Creator of all that exists and happens. It has taken us centuries to grasp the implication that in whatever we can learn of the nature of the universe we are learning something of what God is revealing to us of himself as expressed in his handiwork. For the prophets themselves, and for their successors through many ages, what man could discover for himself by the use of his reason in observation, experiment and reflection was of secondary importance as compared with what was believed to have been said by God to such men as Moses and handed down to be accepted on authority by his people. It is only within the last hundred years, for example, that we have come to the understanding of his method in creation to which I referred at the end of the last chapter.

2. God is thought of as the righteous One who requires righteousness on the part of his people. Here again the implications go far beyond what the prophets themselves are likely to have realized. To them righteousness meant primarily loyalty to Jahweh in the sense of obedience to commandments believed to have been divinely given in the past and handed down as valid for all time. Saul's sparing of Agag would have been a classical example of disobedience and so of unrighteousness.

Nathan's rebuke to David over Bathsheba and Elijah's to Ahab over Naboth mark the beginning of a change. Of the import of this we are only now becoming aware. I know of no better statement of the issues involved than that in three lectures on 'Morality and Religion' given by Dr Clement Webb in 1920.[2] The prophetic principle involves the transition from primitive superstition to the beginning of reasonable religion. If a man wants to know what is the will of God for him he no longer has to cast lots, consult wizards, or simply ask what has been commanded in the past. He has to ask himself what he honestly believes to be the right thing to be done in the circumstances.

How is he to find an answer? He is in parallel case as in that of the method of creation. In matters of 'ought' as well as of 'is' he has to proceed by observation, experiment and reflection; to inspect the circumstances; to see in such men as psychologists, sociologists, and moral philosophers organs of the Holy Spirit through whom God is leading us onward in our moral education; to learn what he can from them as he seeks to see in the circumstances the response for which they call. The foundation of it all is faith in the continued activity of the living God. The one eternal God is the same through all the ages of time. Therefore we rightly look for a consistency in the development of our moral thought, as in each age saints, scholars, scientists, artists, philosophers and others do their best to discern and express his will. Each new suggestion has to be considered in the light of what he has already taught us in the past, while inherited ideas of God have to be revised in accordance with the best moral insight of the present. Of the practical difficulties which this produces much more will have to be said later. The point now is that to refuse to tackle them would be to go back behind the stage at which God inspired the prophets to teach that he is the one Creator whom we must think of as righteous, back from the beginning of reasonable religion into primitive superstition.

3. The prophets shared with their fellow Israelites in the conviction that they were the chosen people of God. There are

[2] Published in *A Century of Anglican Theology* (Oxford, 1923).

passages which teach that this election was not on account of their merit but for the glory of God by his own free choice, and others (especially in second Isaiah) which suggest that it was a call to self-sacrifice on behalf of mankind. But, generally speaking, to be God's chosen people meant to have a superior status in relation to God as compared to others, to be the special objects of his care and protection, to be guaranteed, either in this world or the next, a happy ending to the story of whatever earthly sufferings they are called upon to endure. Sometimes it was the nation as a whole to which this happy ending was promised, sometimes the righteous individual members of it, sometimes both. In any case religion was concerned with the securing of it. For the Deuteronomist Israel must turn away from false gods and seek the favour of Jahweh to be rescued from the nation's enemies. For Ezekiel the wicked man must turn away from the wickedness that he has committed and do that which is lawful and right in order to save his soul alive.

There are thus two inconsistent strains in the prophetic teaching. According to one God's care is for all mankind, indeed for all his creation : Israel, his chosen people, is called to be the instrument through which he wills to work for the rescue of the whole from the toils of evil. According to the other, he has a special care for his own people; his redemptive aim is their rescue from the doom which will befall others and their exaltation to share in his glory. As a result of nearly two thousand years of Christian faith we are accustomed to think of the former as the authentic message which God was seeking through the prophets to bring home to man. But self-concern is an element so deeply ingrained in human nature that two thousand years is all too short a time for man to be able to take in the full meaning of so incredible a word of God. It was preserved in the prophetic writings, and has never been without influence in Jewish and Christian thought. But for the time being it was overlaid by the other strain which, by and large, was taken for granted in the messianic expectations current in the time of Christ.

'Two thousand years is all too short a time.' Do we not still find it only too easy to think of our own salvation as the right and proper aim of our religion, to pray that we may love what God commands in order that we may obtain what he promises? In traditional thought evangelism is the offer of rescue from the doom awaiting unrepentant sinners and efforts to move them to repent and accept it. Many attempts to present biblical theology as *Heilsgeschichte* involve as their central theme this same concern for the saving of a chosen people out of the perishing world. Attempts to expound the doctrine of the atonement are too often bedevilled by concentration on this same issue. When we ask what is the implication of all this for our belief about God the answer must be that what he cares about is the extraction out of his creation of a certain number of men and women for eternal bliss. Is this consistent with thinking of him as the God revealed to us in Jesus Christ?

Looking back over the history of our faith we see the beliefs of our predecessors as part of the history of human thought in which, as I have said, we study 'the human end, the receiving end, of the activity of God the Holy Spirit as he enables men to discount successive layers of presuppositions which colour, and often miscolour, the way they see the truth'.[3] That there should be these misleading presuppositions, this miscolouring, is part of the mystery of evil; that our rescue from them should be by this slow and painful process is part of the mystery of God's redemptive activity. The fact that it takes God so long to free us from identifying religion with concern for personal salvation is evidence of the depth to which self-centredness has penetrated into human nature. What we have seen in the prophetic teaching of the Old Testament is the sowing of a seed which is still struggling to become the greatest among herbs.

[3] See above, p. 12.

We have now two questions to which we must open our eyes as our enquiry proceeds.

1. If human thought is inevitably conditioned by its outlook and men can only grasp so much of the truth as their minds are able to take in, what effect will it have on our understanding of the mind of Christ to realize that the New Testament evidence for it comes to us through the minds of men who shared in one or other of the messianic expectations current in their own time?

2. What will be the effect on our thought about ethics of emphasizing one or other of the two strains in the prophetic thought about God?

II

I have stressed the point, almost *ad nauseum*, that all human thought is conditioned by the outlook of the thinker or thinkers, and that this conditioning has to be allowed for as we study the statements in which their thoughts are expressed. It has this effect on the way in which they express their own thoughts because, in the first instance, it has affected the way in which they have seen things. Whatever objectively may be the nature of what men are looking at, they can only assimilate what their minds, in their present condition, are capable of receiving. Nevertheless, as men with different outlooks compare their respective views errors can be corrected and knowledge grow.

This is God's way of educating men as seen from the human side. One consequence of it is that steps forward have often been due to the work of men who are said to be 'in advance of their time', men who see things that for the time being their contemporaries are honestly quite incapable of seeing. This has happened over and over again in both arts and sciences. As a general rule those who are professional experts in the field concerned are least able to take in at once what the innovator puts before them, and their lack of appreciation delays its acceptance by the wider public. To go no further back than the last century the names of Pasteur and Lister, of Cézanne and Picasso, come at once to mind.

These are tales in which the moral can be clearly seen, for the whole story has been told in less than a hundred years. Our concern is with the moral education of man by God, the eternal God revealing to time-conditioned men a growing knowledge of how he would have them live, a process which has been going on since before the dawn of history, in which we are ourselves involved, which will not be completed before the end of time. As we attempt to understand it we are trying to grasp and expound the significance of contemporary innovations in relation not merely to the thought and practice of the last hundred years but of the whole time span of human history, past, present, and future, in which from our point of view the mills of God appear to grind extremely slowly. During the thousand years or so before the coming of Christ he had got so far as to instil in some men's minds the idea that to be God's chosen people is an enlistment for service rather than a bestowal of status. After another two thousand years, in continuation of the same process, he is opening our eyes to see how this came to fruition in his revelation of himself in Christ.

In the third chapter of Ephesians St Paul (if it was St Paul) speaks of how in Christ God made known a truth which in former times had not been disclosed to the human race but was now revealed by inspiration to 'his dedicated apostles and prophets'. The particular truth he had in mind was that 'through the Gospel the Gentiles are joint heirs with the Jews, part of the same body, sharers together in the promise made in Christ Jesus' (NEB). This had not been immediately obvious to our Lord's own disciples and the first apostles: Galatians and Acts 15 are evidence of how this was an early instance of his promise that the Holy Spirit should lead them further into the

truth and glorify him by finding a way into their minds for
things he had to say which then and there they could not hear
(John 16.12-15). If we believe that the Holy Spirit is still at
work, why may we not believe that he makes use of professional theologians as 'dedicated apostles and prophets' through
whom today he wills to reveal to us some further truth about
Christ which 'in former generations was not disclosed to the
human race'?

'I have yet many things to say unto you, but ye cannot bear
them now.' The more I ponder over the picture of the Lord
Jesus as he emerges from the critical study of the New Testament in the present century, the more convinced I become
that his fundamental difficulty lay in the incapacity of his
fellow Jews to understand his outlook, and that this incapacity
was rooted in the outlook which they had inherited in the
prevalent misunderstanding of what it means to be God's
chosen people. It must not be supposed that the Jews were
unique in thinking of their election as the bestowal of privi-
leged status. If I am right in tracing the origin of religion from
attempts to make personal contact with whatever powers
control the destinies of the universe, it started as an endeavour
to avert the feared enmity of hostile demons, spirits or gods,
or to secure the favour of those disposed to be beneficent. It
was essentially a quest for self-preservation, evidence of the
depth to which already self-centredness had become an ingrained element in human nature. Judaism was not the only
religion to feel stirrings of higher motives. Besides the prophetic voices which spoke of enlistment for service and self-
sacrifice there were those in many lands who saw that human
nature reaches its highest attainable peak when man forgets
himself in devotion to some worthwhile cause, or when he is
drawn out of himself by love of the utterly adorable. But in
spite of the efforts of various philosophers and sages, religion
in general remained the quest for divine favour, for the privi-
leged status which God would give to those who lived lives and

offered worship of the kind that was well pleasing in his sight. In the gentile world at the time of Christ the live religions were various mystery cults which claimed to give to their initiates what were in principle the same benefits as those secured to the duly circumcised and law-abiding worshippers of Jahweh.

Now let us suppose, for the sake of argument, that in thought, word and deed Jesus was the fulfilment of what had been glimpsed of the possible perfection of human character by prophet, philosopher and sage, the man whose concern for himself was completely absorbed in the cause he had come to serve. This is surely the prevailing impression left on our minds by the gospel records, even when we have done our best to discount the influence of any faith in his divinity, when we confine ourselves to asking what kind of a man is left to us by the most rigorous critical study. Witness Bonhoeffer's 'man for others' and van Buren's man who was 'wholly free'. For those of us who think of him as God incarnate it is reinforced by the reflection that such would be the human expression of the kind of love which is constitutive of the godhead. One remembers, for example, Anders Nygren's exaggerated use of his contrast between human *eros* and divine *agape*. The Fourth Gospel rightly interprets the Synoptics when it makes him say 'My meat is to do the will of him that sent me, and to accomplish his work.' He was the actual, historical, human embodiment of the spirit which says 'It doesn't matter what happens to me so long as the Father's will is done.'

Let us suppose further that (whether or no on earth he ever thought of himself as actually God) he believed himself to be sent as God's representative in fulfilment of the messianic prophecies. On what ground did he claim this status? It was derived from his complete devotion to the finding and doing of the Father's will, as standing for God's concerns. The sayings about blasphemy in Mark 3.22-30 and Matt. 12 show that the spirit embodied in 'It doesn't matter what happens to me' carries with it 'I don't mind what you think or say about me so long as you recognize what I stand for as being God's will.' Until a man can see that rescuing another from possession by evil spirits, whoever does it, is doing God's will, there is no hope for him. When the Baptist sent messengers to ask whether Jesus was 'he that should come', he was bidden to draw his own conclusions from what he heard of the work that was being done. The following that Jesus wanted was not that of men drawn by personal devotion to himself, or of those who were concerned about their own salvation, but of those who would share with him in his devotion to the finding and doing of the Father's will.

To Jew and gentile alike this was so utterly incredible that they simply could not take it in. Here was a rabbi claiming to speak in the name of Jahweh, to expound the true meaning of the Mosaic law, bidding them search the Scriptures because they testified of him. It never occurred to them that he could possibly think of religion as not involving concern for God's favour and the soul's salvation, or of these not being the blessings promised to God's elect. This being so, they commonly read into his teachings meanings he never intended, so that over and over again we hear him say 'How is it that ye do not understand?' It is through these men that the gospel records of his life and teaching have come down to us. Inevitably their witness is coloured by the deeply ingrained self-centredness of their religious faith—so deeply ingrained in the human nature of all of us that only now is the Holy Spirit beginning to enable us to disentangle his own idea of God's will for his people from the form in which they have handed it down to us.[4]

We must not forget how central in our Lord's thought was concern for human sinfulness, the conviction that at its heart his messianic vocation was to make the 'full, perfect, and sufficient sacrifice, oblation, and satisfaction for the sins of the

[4] To my mind this disentangling is of greater importance than the comparatively superficial questions of whether they thought in terms of a three-story universe or of God 'up there'.

whole world'. That this was so has been questioned. It has been argued that this interpretation of his mission by St Paul and other New Testament writers had not been in his own mind but was another instance of misunderstanding due to preoccupation with inherited Jewish ideas. I have elsewhere given my reasons for thinking otherwise and will here confine myself to the point that is relevant to the present discussion. The fact that a man should not think of his religion as primarily concerned with his own salvation does not alter the fact that he is a sinner in need of forgiveness and reconciliation to God. It should alter the ground on which he comes to recognize his need. Let a man's eyes be opened to catch a glimpse of God's will for his creation as revealed to us in Christ. Let him be moved to answer the Lord's call to share in his work of overcoming and casting out whatever in it hinders it from embodying and expressing the goodness and glory of its Creator, of setting forward its latent possibilities of such embodiment and expression. Then he will discover for himself how much there is in himself from which he needs to be cleansed and set free, if he is to share in the life of him who was, and is, the wholly free man for others and for God.

What is here involved is an enrichment of our understanding of the doctrines of creation and redemption and of the connection between the two. We have to think of God's care for his creation as a whole instead of concentrating our attention on those whom he wills to save out of it. We have to think of this redemptive activity as geared to the larger purpose.

How do we think of God? We have now reached two conclusions which follow from trying to think of him as the God of the biblical revelation.

1. We learn from the prophets that God is to be thought of as the Creator of the universe who himself is righteous, and that this involves a readiness in every age to revise our understanding of what is his will for us in accordance with such

deepening understanding as he gives us of the moral issues involved in contemporary civilization. To grasp the moral issues it is necessary to understand the situations which give rise to them. We need all the help we can get from historians, economists, psychologists, sociologists and others, all whom God uses as his agents to help us by growing in moral insight to know better how to know and serve him. Among these too are to be found his 'dedicated apostles and prophets'.

2. We learn from Christ that God's righteousness is such as to preclude the thought of him as having favourites or being concerned with the salvation of a certain number of favoured persons out of a perishing universe. He makes the sun to rise on the evil and on the good and the rain to fall on the just and the unjust. He permits men to be massacred by their fellows or accidentally killed by the collapse of buildings irrespective of their degree of sinfulness. In attempting to understand the working of God's providence in history his disciples are to use the same kind of intelligence as in their meteorological forecasts. On the positive side he shows us the kind of things that are of real concern to God: feeding the hungry, healing the sick in mind and body, teaching the ignorant, promoting good cheer at a wedding feast.

We have all the time to be resisting the temptation to read back into our exegesis of the gospel story ideas drawn *a priori* from our belief that it is the story of the incarnate life of God the Son. It is difficult to rid our minds of the thought that he was consciously speaking *ex cathedra*, laying down general rules to be valid for all time as expressions of God's will for man; difficult to remember that this would not have been a genuine incarnation at all. We have to begin by seeing his words and deeds as his response to particular situations, situations arising out of the historical circumstances of time and place. Unique in the fullness of illumination given to his human mind by his union with the Father in the Spirit, his response to each situation was that of a mind so illumined, which expressed the outlook of one conscious of being called to the human fulfilment of his messianic vocation. We have first to see each act and word as the particular response to the particular situation. Then we seek by the guidance of the Holy Spirit to grasp the principle involved in what he did or said and thus to learn what would be the analogous responses required of us in the very different situations in our own lives. When, for example, in Luke 12.13 he refuses to give a ruling on a disputed case of inheritance, we do not take this as meaning that Christians should confine themselves to making generalized statements about covetousness and not concern themselves with the study of questions of economics, jurisprudence and social justice. He had his own messianic work to do and this was outside the range of his professional competence. When in Matt. 19.16-22 he told the rich young man that he should sell all that he had and give to the poor, we do not take this as laying down the ideal practice for all Christians. St Augustine remarked that in his flock those who did so had to be supported by those who did not. It was Christ's diagnosis of the spiritual need of that particular young man as revealed in their conversation.

If we thus begin by narrowing down our exegesis to what was relevant to the original circumstances, the result is not a narrowing but a widening of its relevance for our own guidance. We learn from the second of these two instances that as every human act is a response to a situation the expression of moral judgment must wait upon a patient sifting of the circumstances. From the first we learn the duty of respect for professional standards, that there are cases where the grace of holy orders may not entitle a clergyman to be a better judge of what ought to be done than a layman trained in the social sciences, that we theologians may have lessons to learn from the sociologists.

We can go a step further and consider the application of this to our Lord's ministry as a whole. He saw the world as the Father's world in which he was here to do his best to rescue it from all that prevented the Father's will from being done in it—the Father's will for the welfare, health and happiness of his creatures. He examined each situation on its merits and gave it the careful consideration of an acute and intelligent mind, trying to see what decision would best fit in with his central aim and purpose. He had his own messianic vocation to fulfil. This did not involve engaging in legal practice, economic calculations, political activity, scientific research or many another field of human endeavour. Hence the evidence quoted to the Baptist in justification of his messianic claim was all drawn from within the area of his own doings. He claimed no ability to give technical guidance in other spheres. But the underlying principle is clear. What matters is that each in his own sphere should care first and foremost for the finding and doing of God's will for the welfare of his creation, caring for this so wholeheartedly as to cease to be concerned about his own temporal or eternal destiny.

This was beyond the comprehension of his hearers, of those who accepted his messiahship no less than of those who rejected it. Christianity began as the faith of those Jews who believed that, in spite of all appearances, Jesus of Nazareth had been the fulfilment of the messianic prophecies, and that somehow through his death and resurrection he had won for those who accepted him forgiveness of sin, reconciliation to God, and all the blessings promised to God's chosen people. This was the burden of the first Christian preaching as recorded in the early chapters of Acts. The original Christian gospel was fitted into, and understood in terms of, that current idea of the nature and purpose of religion out of which we are now being led by the Holy Spirit as he takes of the things of Christ and shows them unto us.

At the start, therefore, the basis of Christian ethics was the question: What must we do to be saved? God's redemptive purpose in Christ was taken to be the rescue of those who were to be saved from the destruction to which the rest of creation was doomed. The church was to be a body within which men could receive the benefits of Christ's passion, forgiveness for their sins, and growth in holiness. In its ethical teaching its primary concern was with the kind of life to be lived by its members. For this the ten commandments, reinterpreted as enjoining love of God and neighbour, were the foundation on which succeeding ages have built a great structure of moral and ascetic theology.

No one reasonably can question the value of this, or of its contribution to the ethical thought of mankind. It has been the means of bringing new life and hope to countless sinners, has helped many on the way of holiness, and has gained respect for standards of conduct for which the whole world has been the better. In any revision of our ethical ideas we must take care not to lose the positive gains that have come to us in this tradition. But if we are now being led to see that God's concern is for the welfare of his creation as a whole, and that the first duty of a Christian is to share in that concern, we may reasonably ask whether ethical teaching built on the narrower basis can today meet the needs of either church or world.

It is a world in which good and evil are so interwoven as often to produce situations in which none of the courses open to us is wholly free from evil. Since every human act is a response to a situation, any estimate of its moral quality requires an understanding of the circumstances, a comparison of the possible courses of action and of their relative value. It is God's world in which the church is called to be the continuing earthly body of the risen Christ, through which he carries on his work of finding and doing the Father's will for the welfare of the whole. In its ethical teaching it has somehow to combine the study of how its members may grow in holiness, with that of how both they and others may make the best response that is open to them in the actual situations with which they have to cope.

III

Christian sex ethics are sometimes accused of trying to impose on a world that has come of age outworn restrictive tabus expressing the belief that the sexual element in human nature is something essentially unclean. Despite repeated disclaimers of such manichaeism by Christian theologians this misconception dies hard. Later on I shall call St Paul to witness that it is indeed a misconception, that Christianity came into a world where this evil repute of sex was already widespread in religious circles, that it brought to mankind the secret of its emancipation. I do not suggest that in this respect St Paul himself or any of the New Testament Christians were fully aware of the implications of the gospel any more than in that of the aim and purpose of religion. Christian teaching about sex was fitted into, and understood in terms of, current religious ideas. Again there may be a need of disentangling the true meaning of the gospel from misunderstandings which have persisted too long.

In Matt. 21.31-32 Jesus is reported to have said to the chief priests and elders of the Temple

> I tell you this : tax-gatherers and prostitutes are entering the kingdom of God ahead of you. For when John came to show you the right way to live, you did not believe him, but the tax-gatherers and prostitutes did (NEB).

Until a year or two ago I had always assumed that when he said 'prostitutes' he meant 'ex-prostitutes'. But he is not recorded as having said so. The reason given for their commendation is that they believed the Baptist's teaching about the right way to live. Reference to that teaching in Luke 3 finds no mention of prostitutes. It says that tax-gatherers are to be good honest tax-gatherers, not that they are to cease to be tax-gatherers. The parallel would seem to be that the prostitutes who are entering the kingdom of God are those who are trying to be good honest prostitutes. We have to take into account the present tense of the verb 'are entering'. Our Lord is not talking about what will be the future state of different kinds of people in the world to come; he is describing their present condition in the Palestinian civilization of his time. One may roughly paraphrase him as saying that some tax-gatherers and some prostitutes are ahead of some clergy in the queue for Heaven. Is this a possible understanding of the mind of Christ?

To answer this question one needs a historical investigation into the sociology of that Palestinian civilization. Has the New English Bible made a mistake in using the word 'prostitute' which for us today has discreditable overtones that may not necessarily have gone with the Greek *pornai*? When did the Jews become monogamous—if indeed legally they have ever done so? Was such monogamy as they practised in New Testament times so strict as to exclude all extra-marital affairs? The behaviour of the accusers of the adulterous woman in John 8.1-11 suggests that it was not, and, if not, was there general acceptance of a double standard in the moral judgment on the men who went astray and the women who ministered to their needs? If this was the situation to which Jesus' words were immediately relevant, they may have been meant both to expose the hypocrisy of the double standard and to point out that in a despised class of women there were some who deserved recognition of the value of their contribution to the life of the society of their time.

'The whole of the New Testament,' writes Dr W. G. Cole, 'condemns prostitution or sexual activity of any kind outside marriage, which is considerably more sweeping than the Old Testament wherein the male is allowed a certain limited freedom.'[5] Three questions have to be asked before we can determine the bearing of the New Testament teaching on our understanding of God's will for our sex ethics today. Does

[5] *Sex and Love in the Bible* (London, 1960), p. 318.

'the whole of the New Testament' in this respect accurately interpret the mind of Christ? Is its interpretation coloured by presuppositions drawn from pagan sex tabus? Does it reflect an ethic based on too narrow a concern for those who are to be saved out of this world for the next?

3

CHRISTIAN MARRIAGE:
I. THE NEW TESTAMENT

I

WHAT IS CHRISTIAN marriage? What, indeed, is Christian anything? This wider question must first be considered in the light of what has been said in my first two chapters.

It is no good simply asking what is said about it in the Bible. Both the Old Testament and the New Testament have to be seen in their place in the history of Jewish and Christian thought, and that in its place in the history of human thought in general. When we look back on the course of theological studies in the last hundred years, and set them in their context in general human thought, we see that trends which have been developing over many centuries are now working out to a point at which we are being called upon to make a fresh start in our attempt to understand what Christianity is.

'Faith in the possibility of science,' said Whitehead, 'generated antecedently to the development of modern scientific theory, is an unconscious derivation from mediaeval theology.'[1] That takes us back some six to eight hundred years. For the birth of the 'modern scientific theory' which was to grow out of it there was needed a change of method. This came about in the next two or three hundred years and has been described by Dr Charles Raven as a turning from dependence on the *dicta* of acknowledged authorities in the

[1] A. N. Whitehead, *Science and the Modern World* (New York, 1925), p. 17.

past to study of the *data* provided by the natural world in the present. He showed how modern zoology began when instead of relying on Aristotelian and heraldic representations of animals men based their research on observation of the actual nature and behaviour of living creatures.[2]

We pass on to the coming of the critical study of the Bible in the nineteenth century, through which the scientific impulse generated by mediaeval theology is now preparing to bear fruit in the theology of today. What corresponds to the zoologists' checking traditional definitions by study of actual animals is the theologians' comparison of Scripture and tradition with discoveries made in scientific and historical research. I have already referred to the effect of paying attention to scientific research in our understanding of God's creative activity.[3] For his redemptive work it is history that takes the place of the zoologists' animals.

Theologians, therefore, are at present much concerned with current philosophical discussions of the nature of history, of its status as a science, of the interrelations of fact and interpretation. In *From Bossuet to Newman*[4] Dr Owen Chadwick has given an illuminating picture of theologians haunted by fear of having to build their faith on the shifting sands of historical probabilities. The debate continues. It is as yet too early to foresee its final outcome in agreement among philosophers. Meanwhile too many theologians hanker after an unquestionable basis for faith which shall be immune to either scientific or historical criticism, demanding the kind of revelation they think God should have provided instead of the one he has actually thought fit to give us.

The writing of history, as Professor Nineham has said, involves the confluence of two approaches, the *a priori* argument

[2] *Synthetic Philosophy in the Seventeenth Century: A Study of Early Science* (Oxford, 1945).
[3] Above, p. 19.
[4] Cambridge, 1957. On this see my contribution to *On the Authority of the Bible* (London, 1960), pp. 14ff.

about what surely must have happened and the *a posteriori* argument from the empirical evidence concerning what did happen.[5] The aim of the historian must be a reconciliation of the respective contributions. Once upon a time Aristotle and the Bible provided the *a priori* element. What has taken their place varies in such writers as Paul Tillich, Erich Fromm, John Knox, and Paul van Buren, but it does not excuse their cavalier dismissal of the importance of the empirical *a posteriori*. It is not always easy to discern the source of the *a priori* authority which takes the place of the old infallible Bible. For Fromm it is apparently a Freudian interpretation of human behaviour, for Tillich a form of Hegelian idealism, for Knox reliance on the 'corporate memory of the church', for van Buren the hypothetical contagious influence of a Christ who was 'wholly free'. What they have in common is the assumption that the acknowledged uncertainty involved in historical investigations dispenses them from the laborious task of testing their *a priori* theories by examination of the *a posteriori* evidence. What is the *a posteriori* evidence that van Buren's wholly free man, that Tillich's bearer of the New Being, that Bonhoeffer's man for others and for God, ever actually lived on this earth and was the man that their theories presuppose?

We cannot have it both ways. We cannot preach the gospel as the good news that, in the history of this world, God in Christ has actually taken steps to deal with the problem of evil, and at the same time maintain with Tillich that 'revealed truth lies in a dimension where . . . it is not exposed to critical analysis by historical research'.[6]

We need to see how the biblical studies of the last hundred years dovetail into the movement of thought as we have traced it from its mediaeval impetus through the seventeenth-century checking of traditional authorities by observation of what actually exists and happens. They give us the tools we need for

---

[5] *The Journal of Theological Studies*, April 1958, pp. 14-16.
[6] *Systematic Theology*, Vol. I (London, 1953), p. 143.

observation in the historical field where God's redemptive activity is revealed. Not as yet the answers to our questions, but the tools with which to dig for the answers. They have subjected the books of the Bible, other documents, and archaeological remains to minute scrutiny with a view to discovering their probable date and authorship and the circumstances of their composition—in a word, their provenance. They have gone a long way towards enabling us to understand what was in the minds of those who produced them and what they meant to those for whom they were produced. But the work of enquiring what the truth must have been and be if men such as they were saw it like that still remains to be done. Our historically based understanding of what they did and said is the necessary starting-point for this further study which will, I hope, be the programme for the next phase of theological study.

We shall find it hard to accustom ourselves to the uprooting of traditional habits, as hard as it must have been for the compilers of bestiaries in the early seventeenth century. For so long we have taken it for granted that in the New Testament, in the teaching of Jesus and in the understanding of their faith by St Peter, St Paul, St John and the rest, we have the genuine statement of what Christianity really is; that the subsequent history of the church is the history of a falling away from the original high level of faith and practice; and that what we need is to get back to the understanding of our faith which those New Testament Christians had. It is hard to get used to the fact that in the sense in which we are seeking it they never had it. They were Jews, most of them Palestinian Jews. They had the outlook of their time, place, and culture. Their creed was the Jewish creed of that age. The original Christianity was the faith of a few of them who had followed Jesus of Nazareth in the hope that he might be the promised Messiah. That hope had been shattered by his arrest and execution, revived by his resurrection and transformed into faith that somehow or other, in spite of appearances, he had been the Messiah after all, and was now their heavenly Lord through whom God was carrying out his purpose of reconciling the world to himself. The New Testament shows them trying to make head or tail of what had happened on the basis of their Jewish understanding of God and the universe. So far from having given us a full and final explanation of the meaning of our faith they were taking the first steps towards its discovery, initiating a process which under the guidance of the Holy Spirit has been continuing ever since and is still going on. To answer the question 'What is the Christian view of anything?' we have to take into account how the understanding of it by the New Testament Christians has been deepened and enriched in the experience of their successors, and is still being deepened and enriched by our experience of life in the world of today.

Our starting-point will have to be an attempt to imagine what it would have felt like to be a Palestinian Jew who had come to believe that Jesus had been the Messiah and was now his risen Lord. We must try to picture what would have been the scheme of things that he would have taken for granted, into which the astounding new belief had to be fitted. Then we have to ask what was the new element contributed by this new belief and try to estimate how far its presentation was coloured by the ideas already in his mind, how far those ideas enabled him to grasp its true and lasting meaning, how far they obscured or distorted it, how far deeper understanding was left to be brought to light as in successive ages changing circumstances opened up new avenues of thought.

This illustrates what I have meant by saying that the biblical studies of the last century have brought us to a point at which we are being called upon to make a fresh start in our attempt to understand what Christianity is. The exegetical work of this century has been a necessary preparation. But for too long study of the biblical writers (and, for the matter of that, of patristics, scholastics, reformers and the rest) has been based on the assumption that someone, somewhere, at some time in the past, really knew the truth, that what we have to do is to find out what he thought and get back to it. This seems, for example, to have been the aim of the commentaries on Romans listed on p. 30 of Professor Leenhardt's.[7] The proliferation of this kind of commentary is what must have led a scientist and doctor like Dame Janet Vaughan, in her evidence before the Franks Commission at Oxford, to describe theology as a field of study in which no discoveries of any importance to mankind are likely to be made.

In our study and use of the Bible we need to keep clear in our minds the distinction between exegesis and exposition. The aim of an *exegetical* commentary is to make clear the thought of the writer who is being studied. An *expository* commentary will consider the bearing of his thought on questions at issue in the commentator's own time. The former is a historical study. The criteria to be observed in the scrutiny of the *a posteriori* evidence are those which are proper to that field of enquiry. The attempt must be made to see the writer in his historical circumstances, to interpret his words as relevant to those circumstances, and as expressing the kind of thinking possible to a man of his age and culture. The expository commentator is not conducting a historical enquiry. He is providing material for future historians. He is concerned with the circumstances of his own time, thinking about them with the outlook of a man of his own culture. He has to learn from the exegete what the written word would have meant to its author and his contemporaries, to compare their circumstances and their outlook with his own, and to ask what kind of response to the situations encountered in the world of today would be analogous to that which was made by the writer in the past.

If, starting from the exegetical studies, we look to the Bible for the germs of new ideas which were to grow to maturity as

[7] F. J. Leenhardt, *Epistle to the Romans* (London, 1964).

under the guidance of the Holy Spirit the changing circumstances of successive ages enable men to grow in knowledge of the forms they were to assume, we can look forward to the coming of expository commentaries in which each new generation will be learning what it has to contribute to our understanding of our faith.

This is how we must approach the question of what today should be the Christian way of thinking about sex and marriage.

II

When we try to study the New Testament as source-material for history there are few things more difficult to avoid than reading back our present-day outlook into the minds of its authors and characters. Because for some Roman Catholics Christianity has become the papal church system, they cannot help interpreting texts as though this was the pattern enjoined by Christ on his disciples. For some Lutherans Christianity is essentially the preaching of a certain kind of sermon which produces the response of a certain kind of faith. If this is what essentially it is, this is what it must always have been. The alleged historical facts of the life of Christ are therefore comparatively unimportant. All that really matters was his message concerning the love of God who accepts the unacceptable. When in Acts 8.35 we read that St Philip, finding the Ethiopian eunuch puzzled by a passage in Isaiah, 'preached unto him Jesus', it needs an effort to rid our minds of what that phrase would mean in a present-day evangelistic crusade, to realize that it could only have meant that he must take into his Jewish creed the belief that somehow or other this crucified Nazarene had been the fulfilment of the prophecy and was now his risen Lord and Master.

These are examples of reading into *a posteriori* evidence *a priori* interpretations derived from one's own outlook. We now have to ask whether anything of this kind affects our understanding of New Testament teaching on sex and marriage.

I grew from birth to manhood in a Christian society in which it was taken for granted that monogamy with mutual fidelity of husband and wife was the normal standard expected by God, that among Christians bachelors and spinsters did not have 'affairs', that pre-marital, extra-marital and non-marital sexual intercourse was not done or talked about. It was known, of course, that there were loose-living men, demimondaines and prostitutes, but they were, so to speak, outside the pale. The worldly-wise maxim that a young man must be allowed to 'sow his wild oats' was not acceptable in religious circles, and its extension to young women was unthinkable. It was also taken for granted that these would have been the standards and outlook of both Jews and Christians in the New Testament. Whatever might have been done at earlier stages in Jewish history, God had by this time educated his people up to this moral standard and it was endorsed in the teaching of Jesus and the Christian church.

This understanding of the Judaeo-Christian sex morality in the New Testament was not confined to the circles in which I grew up, as the following quotations show:

By New Testament times polygamy and concubines had begun to disappear from Jewish life and monogamy had almost become the rule.

The whole of the New Testament condemns prostitution or sexual activity of any kind outside marriage, which is considerably more sweeping than the Old Testament wherein the male is allowed a certain limited freedom.[8]

porneia . . . prop. of illicit sexual intercourse in general . . . Acts xv. 20, 29; xxi. 25—that this meaning must be adopted in these passages will surprise no one who has learned from i Cor. vi. 12ff. how leniently *converts from among the heathen* regarded this vice and how lightly they indulged in it.[9]

[8] W. G. Cole, *Sex and Love in the Bible* (London, 1960), pp. 248, 318.
[9] Grimm-Thayer, *Greek-English Lexicon of the New Testament* (Edinburgh, 1892). Italics mine.

If we are not to read back into the New Testament the developed outlook of our own Christian circles, whence can we derive the evidence which will help us to understand what it would have felt like to be living there and then? Again we are driven back to dependence on historical investigation. I began by asking what is the evidence for Dr Cole's statement that among Jews in New Testament times monogamy had almost become the rule and that concubinage had begun to disappear. There is apparently an absence of conclusive evidence, reflected in Dr Cole's tentative words 'almost' and 'begun to disappear'. Moreover I have been told on good authority that monogamy has never become officially a rule of Jewish law : a man is expected to conform to the laws of the land in which he lives. In a Muslim country, for example, he can be a Jew in good standing with wives up to the local legal limit. It would alter our picture of the society in which Jesus moved if we can think of it as containing good Jews with more than one wife, and if the word *pornai* could include respectably recognized concubines as well as professional prostitutes.

We have to look wider afield. We theologians have to get out of the habit of treating the Bible as an all-inclusive source of evidence for the history of God's chosen people. To a certain extent we have learned this lesson. We have learned to take into account the evidence of inscriptions and other archaeological remains. Hebrew and Jewish customs and teaching must similarly be set in the context of the researches of sociologists and social anthropologists. Here I have been helped by the work of Dr Fernando Henriques, who has recently moved from being Lecturer in Social Anthropology at Leeds University to a professorial fellowship at the new University of Sussex. From his survey of the sexual history of mankind[10] four points stand out in my mind.

1. The mating urge, which man has in common with other

[10] *Love in Action: the Sociology of Sex* (London, 1959; references are to the Panther edition, 1964).

animals, is a universal feature in human life. At the human stage in the evolutionary process men and women become consciously and self-consciously responsible for the way in which, both corporately and individually, they run their own lives. Hence they can no longer rely on inherited race habits to guide them to make the best use of their instinctive sexual drives. The problems which arise are human problems and cannot be solved by a policy of 'Back to the jungle'. One remembers the passage from a speech on old age in Plato's *Republic* (329):

In particular I may mention Sophocles the poet, who was once asked in my presence, 'How do you feel about love, Sophocles? Are you still capable of it?' To which he replied, 'Hush! if you please: to my great delight I have escaped from it and feel as if I had escaped from a frantic and savage master.'

These problems are set by the daemonic intensity of the passions that may be aroused. So Henriques writes:

Unrestricted sexual licence cannot be tolerated in society. Its existence would lead to perpetual dissension. On this ground alone it is necessary for sexual relations to be ordered. An equally strong reason . . . is the necessity to assure inheritance of property, and the perpetuation of the society. All these are grounds which apply whatever society occurs. Thus no society exists—or has existed—where general promiscuity is the norm.

Marriage is necessary for the regulation of sexual life and stability in society. What form it takes and what regulations govern the aspirant to matrimony are dependent upon the culture of the particular society. There is no scale of values against which to measure the merits and demerits of different forms of marital union. They must be viewed solely in the context in which they occur.[11]

These quotations from Henriques' chapter on 'Regulation of Sexual Life' show that Judaism and Christianity are not peculiar in requiring respect for restrictive rules and conven-

[11] *Love in Action*, pp. 190, 222.

tions. He gives evidence of the great variety of customs in which, in different times and places, the attempt has been made to reconcile the natural urgency of desire with the needs of social stability. We can accept his statement that any particular practice must be judged in relation to the culture in which it is found, but his apparent denial of the possibility of assessing the relative moral value of differing customs is the kind of scepticism I set out to challenge in my first chapter.

2. The various regulative customs can be classified in three groups distinguished by their sources and aims :

(*a*) Those which are prudential, aiming at the avoidance of civil strife and the safeguarding of property. These are self-explanatory and need no further comment at this stage.

(*b*) Those which express instinctive emotional attitudes that are not consciously related to any religious beliefs. Some of these spring from fear of the terrifying forces involved and are rules of defence against their destructive potentialities. There are also some which express a sense that there is something here which deserves reverence as sacred and private to the individuals concerned. Novelists of today who have abandoned such scruples as a mark of their emancipation from Christian shackles might learn something from Euripides who, in his account of the sacrificial slaying of Polyxena, wrote

> Even as she died
> She took good care to fall full gracefully
> Hiding what should be hid from eyes of men.[12]

This raises the question whether there is not an important distinction to be made between irrational shame rooted in the mistaken idea that sex is in itself something evil, sinful, or nasty and the reasonable shame that has a good part to play in gracious living.

(*c*) Where these emotional attitudes are linked with religious beliefs they take various forms according to the nature

[12] *Hecuba*, 568-70.

of the religion. In some cases the daemonic forces themselves are personified as gods and goddesses who have to be propitiated. More important for our purpose are those where the regulation of sex life is a matter of obedience to the requirements of tribal or national gods or (as in the case of the Jews) of the one and only God. Transgression of the accepted code is sin against God, involving divine disfavour and punishment, disfavour and punishment which may fall upon the whole community unless it takes steps to repudiate the transgressors.

With my scanty knowledge of social anthropology I have not been able to trace the origin of the notion that in sexual activity there is something essentially nasty, unclean and defiling. It may be that it was widespread, and can be found in my group (*b*), apart from any religious belief. Where it is associated with religious belief it produces the idea that sexual activity, whether or no it is exercised in accordance with accepted codes of morality, is in itself unholy and inconsistent with communion with God.

3. It is commonly taken for granted that for men, at any rate, the enjoyment of sexual intercourse with women is a natural necessity for which, as for food and drink, provision must be made. Marriage by itself would not be enough to satisfy the general need. There is a wide variety of customs giving recognition to extra-marital unions, and consequent variety of social status accorded to wives, concubines, and other partners in sexual intercourse. Some men, pursuing a quest for holiness as indicated in 2(*c*) above, might renounce this as inconsistent with their religious vocation and be held in honour by their fellows. But by and large society would think none the worse of men who took advantage of the opportunities offered.

4. One terribly outstanding feature in Henriques' survey is the extent to which, down all the ages, women have been sacrificed to men. In many instances there is the infliction of real cruelty, and one gets the impression that women and

their sufferings are regarded as comparatively unimportant compared with the interests and convenience of men.

The extent to which the personality of women is taken into account as of equal importance with that of men is one of the criteria which Henriques might take note of in attempting to assess the relative moral value of differing customs.

These four characteristics provide the general sociological context within which we have to consider the biblical evidence. Since the publication of *Love in Action* Henriques has been engaged on a more detailed study of *Prostitution and Society*, in the first volume of which he has this to say about it:

While there was official condemnation of sacred prostitution there was no similar disapproval of ordinary prostitution. Such condemnation as there is is concerned more with the effects of consorting with whores leading to economic ruin than with the immorality of such acts.

There is thus a marked difference between Jewish and Christian attitudes towards prostitution. The latter condemns recourse to a prostitute as a sinful act in itself, and financial ruin is subordinate to this. Whereas Judaism reverses the judgment —it is the waste which is the sin.

The lack of prejudice towards harlots as such in Israel meant that their social status was reasonably high.

Hebrew society is thus one where sacred prostitution persists as an alien element for a considerable time. Lay prostitution coexists with it—is evolved within the society itself; foreign influences may have affected its growth but not its origin. Authority was utterly opposed to sacred harlotry as this threatened Judaism itself. On the other hand, ordinary prostitution was tolerated and accepted. This is in complete contrast to the later, Christian attitude which stemming from the Pauline injunctions is one of anathema and condemnation.[13]

How far does this help us towards picturing the Palestinian Jewish society into which Jesus was born, in which he grew up

[13] *The Pretence of Love* (Panther Edition, 1965), pp. 363-4.

and exercised his ministry, and that of the wider Hellenistic world of the Acts and Epistles? It would seem that in both marriage was a socially recognized institution, providing for the security of property and the stability of legitimate family succession from generation to generation. This gave wives an honourable status in society. But there is not sufficient evidence to show whether this was on a strictly monogynous basis or shared between two or more. It did not give wives equality of status with husbands. In Roman law, it is true, a wife could divorce her husband, but this was not so among Jews for whom 'adultery was always intercourse between a married woman and a man other than her husband. A woman could commit adultery against her husband, but a man could not commit adultery against his wife; he could only commit adultery against another married man.'[14]

It looks as though there was recognition of a double standard, as though the physical fidelity required of wives was not generally expected of their husbands, of unmarried men or of widowers. They must have been able to find women who were not other men's wives and so could supply their sexual needs legitimately. It is difficult to assess how far this was an openly acknowledged necessity, and what was the social status accorded to the women who made this contribution to the common life. It is not likely either that they would have been given the same honourable position as faithful wives or that they would all have been socially ostracized as tarred with the same brush. It seems probable that this question would not have been thought of as a deciding factor, that they would have been accepted and able to move at ease in all levels of society for which they were qualified by wealth, manners and accomplishments.

III

According to Mark 10.2-12 and Matt. 19.1-9 Jesus discussed

[14] D. E. Nineham, *St Mark* (Pelican Commentaries, 1963), p. 266.

with some Pharisees the question of marriage and divorce. Reference was made to the Jewish law as laid down in Deut. 24.1-4. This allowed husbands to divorce wives on certain conditions, but rabbis were not agreed on what were permissible grounds. Jesus conceded that Moses had found it necessary to make provision for divorce, but went behind the Mosaic code to Gen. 1.27 and 2.24 which he interpreted as showing that the true fulfilment of God's will would require fidelity in monogamous marriage with no divorce.

This reference to Genesis opens up the whole question of biblical inspiration and interpretation.[15] As a result of our exegetical studies we have ceased to ask what 'the Bible says'. We ask what books or passages meant to their original authors. In many cases this means asking how passages in earlier documents were understood and interpreted in later ones. Now it is probably impossible to discover what would have been in the mind of the original authors of Gen. 1.27 and 2.24.[16] Our starting-point must be the use of them by Jesus. I am not learned enough to know whether in this he was endorsing an interpretation already current among Jewish rabbis or (as often in the Sermon on the Mount[17]) claiming the right to give his own exposition. On Mark 10.11 Professor Nineham comments: 'the teaching . . . will be seen to be strikingly novel, implying as it does that a man *can* commit adultery against his wife. That means that in respect of marriage after divorce both parties are put on a footing of complete equality.'

In any case, in this saying of Jesus we have the basic Christian teaching on the subject of marriage. Here the word 'basic'

[15] On this see my *For Faith and Freedom*, Vol. II, pp. 3-25.

[16] 'It is generally recognized that 24 is not part of the man's utterance contained in 23. To the usual explanation that it is a comment by J it may be objected that such a finished writer would scarcely have been guilty of breaking the thread of his narrative by a didactic notice of this kind. The verse, which suggests a certain reflectiveness (cf. 3.15, 16b) must be deleted as a gloss.' C. A. Simpson, *The Early Traditions of Israel* (Oxford, 1948), p. 54.

[17] E.g. Matt. 5.22, 28, 32, 34, 39, 44.

needs explanation. Those of us who believe that Jesus was God incarnate must not think of him speaking as one conscious of being God, laying down the law for man complete with sanctions to be imposed on those who would disobey it. This would empty of meaning the word 'incarnate'—'was made man'. To have been made man was to have been born as the subject of the experiences of a particular body at a certain time and place in this world's history, to think with the mind and have the outlook of such a one. He was and is the eternal Son, but his sonship was being exercised through the experience of a human life in space and time, his union with the Father in the Spirit taking the form of the illumination of his mind by the Spirit to know the Father's mind and will to the utmost extent open to a man of that age and place. He was speaking to his fellow Jews whose understanding of God's law was that wives must be faithful to their husbands, but husbands were not bound to be equally faithful to their wives. They may or may not have been monogynous, and, according to Henriques, 'the lack of prejudice towards harlots as such in Israel meant that their social status was reasonably high.' He tells them that if they really understood what God was trying to reveal to them through the book of Genesis they would see that the fulfilment of his will for man would require equal fidelity on both sides in monogamous marriage.

Jesus cannot have expected that his hearers would immediately have revised either their law or their practice. Indeed, for the most part they rejected his claim to be the authoritative exponent of God's will. But what of his own disciples, of those who followed him, hoping against hope, and finally came to believe in him as their risen Lord and Master? Why did they include this among the remembered sayings which were thought worthy to be put on record, and what did they think it meant?

It is not likely that upon either the original Jewish Christians or the Hellenistic gentile converts it made such an impression as to bring about an immediate revision of their existing habits of thought and action. That is not the way in which such changes come about. They would surely have gone on observing the laws and customs which in their respective civilizations, Jewish and gentile, provided the accepted standards of morality. To many of them this saying may have been unknown, and those among whom it was preserved may well have been puzzled by it.

We know very little about the disciplinary procedure of the New Testament church:

The first Christians did not think of the Church primarily as an organized society; to them the Church meant the faithful Remnant who were heirs of the divine promises; it was the New Israel comprising God's elect; it was a Temple built of living stones in which the Holy Spirit was present; it was the Body of Christ, composed of innumerable cells, whose corporate task it was to grow in Christlikeness and to bring all mankind into unity with its Lord; it was the sphere of the new creation in which all the barriers of sex, class, race and of sin were transcended.[18]

As in various places Christian churches came to realize that they were bodies professing a new religion distinct from official Judaism, they had to devise their own machinery for the exercise of discipline. We can see the beginning of this in the New Testament,[19] but it was probably not till the second century that it developed into the standardized practice familiar in the patristic age.

The Christians did not invent marriage. It was already there as a social institution, regulated for Jews by Mosaic law, for gentiles by their own laws and customs. Members of the church would be expected to live up to the generally accepted moral standards of society.[20] If we want to know what ideas

[18] J. G. Davies, *The Making of the Church* (London, 1960), p. 34.
[19] E.g. Matt. 18.15-18; Acts 15; I Cor. 6.5; II Cor. 2; I Tim. 1.20; cp. John 9.13-34 for the pattern from which they may have started.
[20] Cp. II Cor. 4.2.

about it were due to the coming of Christianity we have first to ask what would have been already taken for granted by those who embraced the new faith. Originally they would only have been concerned with Jewish law, but as the faith spread through the Mediterranean world problems must have arisen in connection with the requirements of different social traditions. Where they were in conflict, the Christian church, true to its origin, would doubtless have given precedence to the Jewish tradition, but when we ask what it brought in that was new we have to take into account the general climate of opinion in which it was making its way.

Taking all together, there seem to have been in existence three commonly accepted ideas:

1. Whether or no marriage was monogynous wives were required to be faithful to their husbands, but similar continence was not expected of husbands, unmarried men and widowers.

2. Male dominance was taken for granted, whether in the Roman tradition in which wives had been the property of their husbands or in the Jewish summarized by Milton as 'he for God only, she for God in him'.[21]

3. The thought that sex was in some way unclean and defiling, that celibacy was essential to holiness, was widespread in pagan religious circles, and also had a place in the Jewish tradition.[22]

The dualistic type of asceticism which gives rise to this denigration of sex was indeed so widespread and deep-rooted that it has infected the thought of many Christian teachers. St Paul himself was not entirely free from it. But when we ask what in the New Testament is indicative of the *contribution* made by Christianity to the ethics of sex, it is not to that which reflects contemporary ascetic notions that we have to point. Of persons who marry he writes in I Cor. 7.28, 36:

[21] *Paradise Lost*, IV, 299.
[22] Ex. 19.15; Lev. 15; I Sam. 21.4; I Tim. 4.3.

'thou hast not sinned . . . she hath not sinned . . . he sinneth not'. A similar note is struck by the unknown author of Hebrews: 'Marriage is honourable in all, and the bed undefiled' (13.4). The implication is clear. Christianity proclaims the possibility of freeing the sex relationship from every taint of uncleanness or sin.

Eph. 5.22-33 may or may not be by St Paul. The fact that wives are exhorted to be in subjection to their husbands is of little or no importance. No moralist of that age could have said anything else. But verses 25-31 contain the germ of an idea so startling that whoever wrote it had to confess that he could not take in all its implications and said 'This is a great mystery'. 'Husbands, love your wives, even as Christ also loved the church and gave himself up for it.' Whether or not at the time the writer or his readers could have grasped so incredible a suggestion, it sounded the death knell of male dominance in marriage. For the Christian the figure of Christ on the cross is the supreme example in history of 'what love might be, hath been indeed, and is'. What bride and bridegroom are to promise in their marriage vows is that they will build a joint life in which each will daily lay down his or her life for the other.

In the teaching of Jesus and the New Testament Church the seed is sown which is to bear fruit in the transformation of the idea of marriage. It is to be a monogamous union maintained by mutual fidelity in a partnership of equals, a union which gives bodily expression to love after the pattern of that made manifest in Christ, in which there is nothing in the enjoyment of its physical ecstasy which is inconsistent with holiness and communion with God. I emphasize the analogy of the sowing of a seed, for this is characteristic of the method of God's redemptive work in Christ. He came as man to work from within the history of this world by winning men and women to share with him in seeking to find and know the Father's will and give themselves in its service. Sex, like everything else in creation, was essentially good. Its infection by evil was due to its misuse. Its rescue must be wrought from the inside, by men and women who would discover what could be made of it when enjoyed in accordance with God's will.

The world being what it was, this was the beginning of a long process which is still going on. There are passages in the Pastoral Epistles which suggest that while monogamy was required of candidates for the office of deacon, presbyter or bishop, this was not so for the general body of the laity.[23] There are many passages in patristic and later writings which show how deeply Christian thought had been infected with the notion that in sex there is something unclean and defiling, and some special holiness attaching to celibacy and virginity. Indeed we are still not wholly free from those prejudices, any more than from those which imagine that the truly religious man should be concerned about the salvation of his soul, or think of the church as the ark of salvation.[24]

[23] I Tim. 3.2, 12; Tit. 1.6. If so, the practice of the New Testament church may have some relevance to questions raised by polygamous civilizations in Africa. See above, pp. 17, 18.
[24] See above, p. 27.

4

CHRISTIAN MARRIAGE: II. TODAY

I

FOR AN ANSWER to the question, 'What is Christian Marriage?' we have both to examine its nature at the time of its introduction and to trace its development through the nineteen hundred years of Christian history with a view to seeing what is becoming of it today. Having learnt from sociologists something of how civilized society has always required some kind of regulation of human sexual activity, I have tried to set the New Testament references to the subject in the context of the methods of such regulation then prevailing. I propose now to pass immediately to the conditions of the present time, only referring to the intermediate history when that is necessary to consider how developments have come about.

It would take too long to try to give a catalogue either of all the regulative laws and customs now obtaining in different lands, or of all the various proposals put forward for their improvement. I will content myself with saying that from what I have heard and read of them these proposals seem to fall into three main groups.

A. It is sometimes suggested that the trouble is due to our attaching an exaggerated importance to what should be treated as a routine matter of physiological process. We should arrange to satisfy our sexual needs with no more fuss and bother than are ordinarily associated with our daily meals. It is not our nature that is the cause of our disquiet but our way of thinking about it.

I need not now pause long over this suggestion, though I shall have something more to say about it in the next chapter. It represents a very natural reaction against a counter tendency to over-emphasize the importance of sex. It is attractive to the children of parents who have a manichaean horror of sex as something nasty and unclean. At the opposite extreme it may also express an attempt to 'cut sex down to size' by some who are weary of hearing its enjoyment extolled as the one thing worth while and rebelliously declare that there must be something else worth living for. But it ignores the sociologists' recognition of the necessity of regulating human sexual activity. In all probability there would never have been either the manichaeans or the others if man's sexual nature had not refused to be ignored as an imporant psychological and moral factor.

B. The second type of suggestion fully recognizes all this. Sexual intercourse is to be the expression of genuine affection, the 'sacramental' consummation of deep and intimate friendship. It is degraded whenever exercised in the absence of such attachment as, for example, in commercial prostitution or the fulfilment of uncongenial marital obligations. Just because this reduction of sexual intercourse to the satisfaction of bodily needs is its degradation, lifelong monogamy must be condemned along with commercial prostitution, promiscuity, and all forms of type A. Such friendships as rightly seek for this consummation may arise in various directions in the course of a single life. Moreover, any particular one may fade away, in which case the continuance of a 'married life' which had been based upon it may itself become an offence against the best standards of living. Where there are children marriage may be justified as providing them with home life and the care of two parents; but it must clearly be understood that the association of father and mother for the purpose of rearing their family does not require them during this period to enjoy with each other, and only with each other, the consummation of romantic friendship. The great obstacle to right living is the evil passion of jealousy which leads lovers, husbands, and wives to make unjustifiable demands for exclusive rights in their partners. To curb one's generous capacity for varied friendships is an evil constriction of what is best in human nature, but to free oneself from jealousy is to be rid of a base and corrupting influence. Happiness will come to the human race when it has learned to cast out jealousy and to allow the fullest possible liberty for sexual intercourse as the expression, freely willed on both sides, of deep affection.

Such suggestions cannot be condemned outright or dismissed in a hurry. They represent a genuine and serious attempt to solve one of the chief social problems of civilized man, an attempt not to overthrow but to improve morality. They aim at raising the tone of society by turning men and women away from subservience to bodily desires, teaching them to use their bodies as instruments for deepening love and to accept responsibility for the welfare of possible children. They claim to provide a reasonable basis for self-control by not requiring it except where it is reasonably necessary, and to be guiding mankind aright in directing our disapproval on its proper object, jealousy. But whether experimentation on these lines would lead to the discovery of the ideal way of life is open to question, and that for at least three reasons.

(i) It is probable that for women as well as for men the desire for sexual satisfaction is not the same thing as the desire for parenthood. But it is doubtful whether in the long run any permanent satisfaction of sexual desire can be attained unless its fulfilment is woven into some enduring creative activity. Sooner or later there comes a weariness of consummating one romantic friendship after another, a disillusionment with life which has not provided what was expected of it. The pursuit of happiness through successive romantic unions turns out to be the pursuit of a will-o'-the-wisp.

(ii) It is doubtful whether the casting out of jealousy in the manner suggested is either possible or desirable. The self-control necessary to overcome it is hardly likely to be promoted by relaxation of self-control in other directions. And if jealousy is to be removed by removing its ground in the desire for some special and exclusive relationship, it is questionable whether the affection of those who do not care enough for each other to care about this will be as 'romantic' as is supposed. Can depth and richness of sexual love be achieved without jealousy? Can the depth and richness be retained, and the jealousy be at the same time overcome, by any other method than mutual trust and faithfulness?

(iii) It is doubtful whether liberty to consummate friendships in this way is necessary for the development of a wide and rich experience of human relationships between men and women. Might it not, indeed, have the opposite effect? There is a good deal of evidence that it is where such possibilities are ruled out by mutual consent that the doors are opened for the most fruitful co-operation.

c. The third group is the one within which Christian thought finds itself at home. It agrees with the second that sexual intercourse should be the sacramental consummation of deep and intimate friendship, but it holds that it can only fulfil its possibilities as consummation if that consummation is itself the beginning of something more, if it is taken up into the living of a joint life of creative activity.

The word 'consummation' is misleading. It conveys a suggestion of finality, of something which is valued as an end in itself. There is truth in this. It has got a value in itself as an expression of love in a joyful union which involves the whole human self, spirit, soul and body. But it is not the whole truth. This which is the consummation, the climax, and the end of one stage in the relationship, can be the beginning, the source from which something greater can grow. How this can be done is the lesson we are still in process of learning as we try to follow up the initial impetus given by the New Testament insights.

One of those insights was that the love which was to find expression in marriage should be of the same kind as the love of Christ for his church. There are two sayings of Jesus which have to be taken together when we think about the nature of love. We are to love the Lord our God with all our heart and soul and mind and strength and our neighbours as ourselves, and 'Greater love hath no man than this, that a man lay down his life for his friends.'[1]

The first of these sayings implies that the love he has in mind is a devotion which involves the whole personality. 'Heart, soul, mind and strength' are the words there used. We are more accustomed to speak of the feeling, thinking and willing self. In the second saying there is no explicit reference to either feeling or thinking. The whole emphasis is on what is *done*: *'that a man lay down his life'*. Why is this? Let it be granted that perfect love would be the devotion of the whole self. But we men and women are not perfect. Our love is often defective in one way or another. Our devotion may be defective in any one or more of our three activities. If it is defective in thinking it may lead us to do very silly things. If it is defective in feeling it may produce a very ugly contentment with behaviour held to be in accordance with Christian charity. If it is defective in willing it may exhaust itself in expressions of sentimentality which get nothing done. Of these three it is the willing, the action, which is most immediately under our control. Our feelings come and go and are not always at our command.[2] We may, so far as thinking is concerned, be at the mercy of invincible ignorance or ingrained stupidity. But what we are responsible for, being the people we are with the feelings and thoughts that we have, is what we decide to do.[3] We are not to rest content with a love which is anything less than

[1] Mark 12.30, 31; John 15.13.
[2] More than forty years ago when I was lecturing on this subject a street organ outside the window began playing 'You made me love you: I didn't want to do it.'
[3] On this, see my *For Faith and Freedom*, Vol. I, pp. 139ff.

the devotion of the whole self. When we find it difficult, if not impossible, to think and feel as we ought, we must not let that be an excuse for acting wrongly.

Correct action, as I have said, when it is not the expression of love which is felt, may be a very horrid thing. But there are circumstances in which it may be the best that we can do. Then it can only be saved from becoming that very horrid thing if we realize the danger, deplore our defectiveness as already horrid, and pray for the grace of God to enable us to love with the heart as well as with the will. The realization of the danger, and the recognition of our defectiveness and of what we need to pray for, are the contribution of the mind.

In the civilization of the western world at the present time, when we think of love it is usually the element of feeling that is most prominent in our mind. From the sociological point of view the purpose of marriage is the regulation of sexual activity. Doubtless it is the strength of the passions generated by such feelings which have made the regulation necessary to civilized life, but the evidence is against the view that in general marriage has been regarded as making adequate provision for their control or, indeed, as necessarily having any connection with love. The stability of society and the safeguarding of property have been the primary concern. If husband and wife could satisfy their mutual need of love, well and good. If not, for the husband at any rate, there were others to whom he could turn.

It is possible that, whether or no he knew what he was doing, the author of Ephesians introduced a new principle in suggesting love of any kind as the essential basis of marriage. Certainly down the ages of Christian history the acceptance of it has been slow to develop. Marriages have continued to be arranged to further dynastic or family interests. The claim of romantic love to make a valuable contribution to human living has had to win recognition. I shall not attempt to trace the details of its history. The upshot of it is that today we commonly take it for granted (i) that marriages should be based on love and (ii) that love is pre-eminently a matter of feeling.

(i) That husband and wife should love one another was included in the New Testament teaching which gave the initial impetus to Christian thought and practice. But it is not likely that the existence of such mutual love would have been regarded as the standard basis on which marriages would be arranged. It was something which husbands and wives, whatever the original ground of their union, must seek by the grace of God to develop within their marriage. Today we assume that there is something wrong with a marriage contracted otherwise than by the free consent of a man and a woman on the basis of their already existing mutual love. We may have to admit that too often circumstances necessitate such unions, shrug our shoulders, hope for the best, and pray that the grace of God may be as potent now as in New Testament times. One question we have to face is whether the shift of emphasis by which love is made the pre-existent ground for entering upon marriage is a right development of Christian thought or an unfortunate instance of deviationism.

(ii) This shift of emphasis is complicated by the tendency to treat the element of feeling as the chief constituent in the romantic love which is to be the basis of marriage. It has its roots in our physical nature, and while scientists may be able to discover why particular persons are physically attractive or repulsive to one another, either hetero or homosexually, for practical purposes we have to start from the fact that this is what happens. A man and a woman may find that the presence of the other stirs thrills in any or all of their five senses, desire for closer contact, and longer association. The love which has its roots in the physical attraction may or may not be a plant which produces community of interests in matters of mind and will. If it is, one of two things may follow. The pursuit of these common interests may absorb the attention while their rootage is to all intents ignored or forgotten. Or it may be enriched as the fruit of an origin which reaches its consummation in physical sexual intercourse.

In no stage of its growth, so far as we have considered it, does this love demand the lifelong exclusive companionship of one man and one woman. This is the problem which faces all adherents of monogamy who hold that marriage should be based on and be the expression of love. It leads some of them to give it up, to say that things were better when marriages were arranged on other grounds and monogamous fidelity maintained by the control of feelings in accordance with God's law. As an alternative to this attempt to turn back the clock I want now to suggest that the emergence of so-called romantic love has had a valuable contribution to make to our growing understanding of what Christian marriage should be, a contribution of which we can reap the benefit if, instead of either exaggerating or belittling the element of feeling, we welcome it in such a way as to enable it to play its full part in a love which is the devotion of the whole personality.

The first thing necessary is that these sexy feelings of physical attraction should be welcomed as given by God for the enrichment of human life. Next we must accept the fact that, though perhaps it may sometimes occur, it is unusual for any particular man or woman only to have them in relation to some one particular partner. In the course of a lifetime they may be the source of multiple enjoyment in many different relationships. To refuse to enjoy them is ingratitude to God's generosity; to pretend that the enjoyment is not sexy offends against his care for truth; to think that it is something to be ashamed of is to criticize his creative wisdom. How, then, can a stable and enduring union be built upon so fluctuating a foundation? The answer surely is that the romantic element of feeling will only come to its fullness if it is taken up to play its part in harmony with our thinking and willing selves in a partnership directed towards some outward looking end or ends.

In the grip of romantic passion two people may feel that life has nothing more to offer than that they should continue endlessly to gaze into each other's eyes and satisfy their desire to be united. But there is abundant evidence that taken as an end in itself this satisfaction has no guarantee of endurance. That is why I speak of 'some outward looking end or ends'. The deepest and most enduring ties of affection and love are forged when men and women are drawn together in the pursuit of some interest or cause which draws them out of themselves into shared devotion to a common aim. This is where the thinking mind has its part to play, asking whether this particular sexual attraction is one which has promise of coming to fruition as the enrichment of two lives joined in such pursuit of shared interests. Then the marriage is sealed with the act of will when the two vow that they will lay down their lives, each for the other and both jointly in the service of God and their fellow men.

Ideally the Christian priest should be able to say to bride and bridegroom: 'You have received from God this gift of joy in one another. In it you have heard his call to a joint life in his service. Never forget that your joy in one another's bodies is his gift and that it will give him pleasure to see you enjoying it to the full. But never forget also that it is yours to enjoy as an element in that joint life of service to which you have now taken your vows.'

'Greater love hath no man than this, that a man lay down his life for his friends.' 'Thou shalt love the Lord thy God with all thy heart and soul and mind and strength.' 'This is a great mystery: but I speak concerning Christ and the church.' This last quotation suggests an analogy between the love of husband and wife and the Christian's love for God which is to be the devotion of the whole self, 'heart, soul, mind, and strength'. This does not always, but does sometimes, start with a felt experience:

God was suddenly someone experienced, asserting with ten-
derness, the beauty and strength of which nearly annihilated
me altogether, that I was loved and I was forgiven. It is almost
impossible to explain to a non-Christian what this experience
consists of, nor why it changes every relationship and every
attitude. Abelard came nearest to expressing the heat and the
passion of it. . . .[4]

It is the agreed testimony of the mystics, and of others with
knowledge and understanding of Christian spiritual life, that
the presence or absence of such experiences is not to be taken
as an index of man's progress in the love of God. One and all
they speak of periods of dryness, which they interpret as
periods in which they are being put to the test of discovering
whether they love God for himself or for the enjoyment they
get out of it. We should accept with gratitude all such joyful
experiences as God may give us, but to be faithful in service
when all feeling is dead is the mark of one who truly loves
God and is the path of spiritual progress.[5]

Mutatis mutandis we may apply these thoughts to the vows
taken by a Christian bride and bridegroom before the altar.
'To love and to serve till death us do part.' God has brought
them there through the feeling that they have for each other.
But if they have thought that what the church expects them
to do is to go on consistently feeling like that for the rest of
their lives they should have been taught to get any such silly
idea out of their heads. This is where the saying 'Greater love
hath no man . . .' comes in, the saying which is concerned
not with feeling but with action. In some exceptional cases
the laying down of one's life may mean actually dying. Far
more often it means being faithful in service. What the bride

[4] Monica Furlong, *With Love to the Church* (London, 1965), p. 84.
[5] Cp. 'For it is the commonest principle of Christian prayer that, in
times of aridity and lack of fervour, in times of "non-religion", the disciplines of sacrament and divine office are more necessary not less, more
creative not less, more genuine expressions of love for God, a more real
response to grace.' Martin Thornton, *The Rock and the River* (London,
1965), p. 63.

and groom are called upon to vow is that day by day, come good fortune or bad, they will be faithful in their service of one another and their joint service of God and man. For them, too, the time may come for the depth of their love to be tested by trial of their perseverance in that service when feeling is dead, when all they can do is to go on laying down their lives while in faith and hope they wait upon God for the restoration of the kind of love with which he had first brought them together.

Faced by the sociological necessity of regulating sexual activity Christianity proposes that the best way of doing this will be by the harmonious co-operation of feeling, thought, and will in a lifelong monogamous union. It is not trying to maintain an old-fashioned institution which the world is in process of outgrowing, but is commending to mankind a way of dealing with the problem which has to its credit a record of substantial success. So much so, indeed, that marriage of the Christian type has come to be commonly regarded as the normal standard to be aimed at in western civilization. It has come to be thought of, not as the fruit of Christian faith and practice, but as something which can be required by legislation of any and every one. Christianity is regarded as laying upon men's backs burdens too heavy to be borne rather than as offering initiation into a way of life, commending to the world and establishing among men and women that way of living their sexual life which experience shows to have most hope for the future.

II

We today have to think of the part to be played by love in marriage in a way that would have been impossible for anyone in the time of St Paul. Through the ongoing history of our civilization our eyes are being opened to a fuller understanding of the revelation of God in Christ. Now, besides welcoming the contribution made by our learning to value romantic love, we must consider the bearing of change in the relative status of men and women in society on that of husband and wife in marriage. Here may be another instance of the Holy Spirit seeking, through the work of sociologists, to take of the things of Christ and declare them unto us. Compare, for example, the following traditional exposition of Pauline teaching by a theologian with a sociologist's account of present day conditions:

God establishes an ordinance in which you can live together as man and wife. 'Wives, be in subjection to your husbands, as is fitting in the Lord. Husbands, love your wives, and be not bitter against them' (Col. 3.18, 19). With your love you are founding a home. That needs an ordinance, and this ordinance is so important that God establishes it himself, for without it life would be reduced to chaos. You may order your home as you like save in one particular: the woman must be subject to her husband, and the husband must love his wife. In this way God gives to man and woman the glory peculiar to each. It is the glory of the woman to serve the man and to be a 'help meet' for him, as the creation story calls it. And it is the glory of the man to love his wife with all his heart. He 'will leave his father and mother and cleave to his wife', he will 'love her as his own flesh'. A woman who seeks to dominate her husband dishonours not only him but herself as well, just as the man who does not love his wife as he should dishonours himself as well as her, and both dishonour the glory of God which is meant to rest upon the estate of matrimony. There is something wrong with a world in which the woman's ambition is to be like a man, and in which the man regards the woman as the toy of his lust for power and freedom. It is a sign of social disintegration when the woman's service is thought to be degrading, and when the man who is faithful to his wife is looked upon as a weakling or a fool.[6]

Women ultimately achieved political equality with men, and, at least to a greatly increased extent, a measure of effective social equality with men. Women have thus come to possess recognized rights in owning and managing property, in

* Dietrich Bonhoeffer, *Letters and Papers from Prison* (London, 1954; Fontana Edition, 1964), p. 151.

educational opportunity, in entry to many occupations, and in sharing to the full extent that their inclinations, abilities, and circumstances will allow in public, social, professional and wage-earning work. Women now enter marriage on a completely voluntary basis and on an equal footing with their male partners. This improved status has meant, of course, that many women no longer wish to be confined to a life of child-bearing, child-rearing, and domesticity, but wish—sometimes instead, sometimes in addition—to go out to work and to pursue whatever aims and interests they might have.

In the modern marriage, both partners choose each other freely as persons. Both are of equal status and expect to have an equal share in taking decisions and in pursuing their sometimes mutual, sometimes separate and diverse, tastes and interests. They live together permanently and intimately in their own home and in relative independence of wider groups of kindred. They base their choice in marriage and the maintenance of their subsequent relationship on personal love. With equality of status and mutuality of consideration they desire full 'compatibility' in marriage. The marital relationship has thus come increasingly to be considered as something worthwhile in and for itself.

The changed position of women is of particular importance here. With the improvement in the education and in the occupational opportunities of women, with their equal right to pursue their interests and develop their talents, with the practice of birth control, and also with the extended expectation of life, the position of the woman in the family has been changed more fundamentally than many realize.

The husband portrayed by previous social investigators is no longer true to life. In place of the old comes a new kind of companionship between man and woman, reflecting the rise in status of the young wife and children which is one of the great transformations of our time. There is now a nearer approach to equality between the sexes and, though each has a peculiar role, its boundaries are no longer so rigidly defined nor is it performed without consultation.[7]

[7] R. Fletcher, *The Family and Marriage* (Penguin Edition, 1962), pp. 109, 130, 131, 145. The last passage is quoted by Fletcher from Young and Willmott, *Family and Kinship in East London* (London, 1957).

As a matter of straight exegesis Bonhoeffer represents what would probably have been in the mind of St Paul. It would be unreasonable to expect any moralist of his age to question the rightness of male dominance in marriage. The best he could do was to seek to have it tempered by the husband's love. When we set his teaching in the context of the whole history of relations between the sexes we cannot forget the extent to which the interests of women have been subordinated to those of men, the hideous cruelties that have been inflicted. This tempering of dominance by love was a forward step in a long process of righting intolerable wrongs. It was, moreover, a step which prepared the way for a further advance far beyond anything that St Paul himself could have foreseen.

When Christian husbands were told to love their wives 'even as Christ also loved the church and gave himself up for it', this was in a passage which gave the husband lordship over his wife parallel to that of Christ over his church. We may question whether the injunction to love with a love after the pattern of the love of Christ for the church should involve for all time the kind of lordship of husband over wife which was then read into it. We think of Christ as the Lord of whom it was said that he 'being in the form of God, counted it not a prize to be on an equality with God, but emptied himself, taking the form of a servant . . . and being found in fashion as a man he humbled himself'. According to the Johannine account he had said:

This is my commandment, that ye love one another even as I have loved you. Greater love hath no man than this, that a man lay down his life for his friends. Ye are my friends if ye do the things which I command you. No longer do I call you servants, for the servant knoweth not what his lord doeth: but I have called you friends, for all things that I have heard from my Father I have made known unto you.

Whatever may or may not have been in the mind of St Paul we can now see that if any kind of lordship is to be given to the husband it is not that of the risen ascended Christ over his church, but of the incarnate Lord who, when bidding his disciples to love one another even as he had loved them had put himself on an equality with them. He could not have been bidding them to lord it over one another.

According to Bonhoeffer's exposition of Pauline teaching the Bible presents us with a divine ordinance for the ordering of family life in which the relative positions of husband and wife are fixed for all time. This belongs to the stage of theological study at which the Bible is held to be legislating for the affairs of the community with ordinances of timeless validity to which sociological changes are irrelevant.[8] The case is altered when we see the whole of human history as God's education of man in the art of how to live, God caring above all for man's growth in the right use of his freedom and the Bible as bearing witness to the way in which his redemptive activity contributes to the fulfilment of his creative purpose.

The gospel then becomes the proclamation that by his death and resurrection Christ set men free to grow in fuller understanding of what he stood for as God's will for man, to go on learning more and more of the many things which he still has to say to his disciples, which they could not then take in.[9] No one surely can look back over the whole history of human society without recognizing it as a God-inspired ethical advance when 'women ultimately achieved political equality with men, and, at least to a greatly increased extent, a measure of effective social equality with men'. It is analogous to the transition from Jacob's standards of honesty to those of Psalm 15.[10] We must not forget what Bonhoeffer rightly stood for when he said that those who marry are founding a home, and that if life is not to be reduced to chaos there is needed a *modus vivendi* in which husband and wife can each play the

[8] Cp. the section on 'The Four Mandates' in his *Ethics* (Fontana Edition, 1964), pp. 207ff.
[9] John 16.12.   [10] See above, p. 13.

part appropriate to their sex. This differentiation of sexual capacity and function is recognized by Fletcher, and Young and Willmott, when they claim for women a sharing of social life and responsibility 'to the full extent that their inclinations, abilities and circumstances will allow', speak of husband and wife 'pursuing their sometimes mutual, sometimes separate and diverse, tastes and interests' and in welcoming a 'nearer approach to equality between the sexes' add that 'each has a peculiar role'. But the order which is to prevent chaos is to be maintained by 'mutuality of consideration' by husband and wife, who 'both are of equal status and expect to have an equal share in taking decisions'.

Can this be done? And if so, how? We are at a stage in the history of Christianity and of marriage in which God is calling on us to discover how by his grace we may be enabled to make the sociologist's dream come true. 'They base their choice in marriage and the maintenance of their subsequent relationship on personal love. With equality of status and mutuality of consideration they desire full "compatibility" in marriage.'

III

A practical problem is now presented to the Christian church. If Christian ethics were the application of rules laid down once and for all in Scripture, or by some authority in the past, the provision of a code of discipline for the regulation of sexual life might be a fairly simple matter. But if we are in process of being led by the Holy Spirit to learn more fully what Christian ethics should involve in the circumstances of our time, it is not so easy. This learning is not just an intellectual exercise of study, thought, discussion and argument. Intellectually, as theory, the hypothesis is that human sexual energy will achieve its true fulfilment and make its best contribution to social life by finding expression in the lifelong monogamous union of man and wife joined together in equal partnership in the service of God and man. Its experimental verification can only come by the self-discipline of Christian men and women who hear God's call to try to live by it and so prove to themselves and to the world that by his grace it can make good its claim. How can the church recognize that it is engaged in this experiment and at the same time prescribe rules for its members which do not assume in advance that its conclusions have been proved?

This problem will need a chapter to itself. Meanwhile in order to grasp it completely we cannot leave the subject of marriage without considering divorce.

We are trying to learn what Christian marriage should be in the context of our present civilization and we must try to do the same with divorce. We have seen how St Paul introduced a new note in his teaching about how a husband should love his wife, and how Jesus introduced a new note in saying that a husband can commit adultery against his wife as well as a wife against her husband.[11] His statement that remarriage after divorce is a form of adultery clearly implies that for Christians marriage should be a lifelong monogamous union. But the question remains whether, owing to the 'hardness of men's hearts', there can still be allowable exceptions. This is again the kind of question for which the theologian has to ask how far psychological and sociological studies may help us to learn what would be the mind of Christ for us today.

Two actual incidents may help to set the scene.

(a) During the 1914-1918 war an Australian soldier on service in Europe met and married an English girl. He went back to be demobilized, find work, and make a home for her to come out to. She turned out to be a thoroughly bad lot: during the journey out she had affairs with various men on the boat and after she had joined him her behaviour was such that he divorced her. He then went out to start a new life in one of the South Pacific islands. There he met a woman who was a

---

[11] See above, p. 51.

believing and practising Christian, one of the mainstays of the local church community. They fell in love with one another and the question of their possible marriage was put before the bishop. He declared that he could not rightly allow the unfortunate incident in the man's past to be a barrier to their founding a home which would be a source of strength to the church in the island.

(b) Between thirty and forty years ago I was talking in New York to a woman who lived in one of the residential New Jersey suburbs. She told me of a neighbour whose wife had deserted him and gone off with another man. He sold his house and went to live in a club. Some few years later he tired of club life, thought he would like to have a house of his own again and bought one. The rumour went round that he must be going to marry again. My friend told me that one day she met him in the street and decided to ask him straight out if this was true. 'He looked at me,' she said, 'with a look that seemed to wither me, and replied "I thought *you* would have understood that when I married my wife I took my vows to God; no matter what she may have done those vows stand".'

Those two incidents have remained in my memory as clear cases, at opposite ends of the spectrum, where straightforward decision is possible. I cannot dispute the rightness of the bishop's decision in the first, and yet I would not say anything that might diminish the respect and, indeed, admiration due to the deserted husband's resolution in the second. The difficulty lies in the fact that the great majority of the cases fall somewhere between the two.

Dr Maude Royden once said one of the wisest things that I have heard on this subject: that we shall get things right only when husbands and wives come to think and feel about their marriage as a sea captain thinks and feels about his ship. Now government agencies, such as our Board of Trade, make rules and regulations designed to ensure that, so far as is possible, when a ship sets out from port it shall come safely to the end of its journey. If there should be a shipwreck, then an enquiry will be held with a view to discovering who, if anyone, was to blame, whether anything can be done to prevent a recurrence of the disaster, and how best as much as possible can be saved from the loss of the vessel. But no government in its senses has ever tried to draw up in advance a list of rules for permissible shipwrecks.

The present practice of the Church of England seems to me to correspond pretty well to this pattern. In the wedding service the bride and bridegroom undertake to have the same kind of care for their marriage as the captain undertakes when he is entrusted with the command of his ship.[12] If subsequently the marriage breaks down and there is a separation or divorce, we have to ask how best as much as possible can be saved from the loss. From conversation with various bishops I know how often they are asked for rulings concerning the admission to communion of divorced and remarried members of the church. Probably there are few cases as clear as that of the Australian soldier. There must be many which are like those of which Miss Furlong has written: 'I can think of divorces where not merely one but both of the parties have achieved a happiness and fulfilment they could never have achieved with the first partner.'[13]

[12] How many of them, as a matter of fact, understand what they are supposed to be doing may be open to question. What is needed here is not a change of theory or fresh legislation but better pastoral care.

[13] *With Love to the Church*, p. 53.

5

THE CHURCH IN THE WORLD

I

STARTING FROM THE revelation of God in Christ, the Christian church is in process of discovering the best way of weaving human sexual energy into the fabric of a life worth living. This discovery has required, and still requires, the combination of two lines of approach: the attempt to enter into the mind of Christ by reflection on the records of his earthly ministry, and, in each age, the attempt to live by what so far has been discovered in the circumstances of the contemporary world. As we study the works of our ancestors, from the biblical writers through the patristics, scholastics, reformers and the rest, we have to consider how each has been helped or hindered in his understanding of the mind of Christ by his attempt to relate it, in thought and practice, to the psychological and sociological conditions of his time and place. Through its interaction with the world the church, on the basis of the revelation of God in Christ, is engaged in the discovery of what its sexual ethics should be. Our task today is to carry on this work as twentieth-century theologians of the western world.

> For life, with all it yields of joy or woe,
> And hope and fear—believe the ancient friend—
> Is just our chance o' the prize of learning love,
> How love might be, hath been indeed, and is.

I have suggested that the positive contribution made by Christianity has been a way of thinking about and engaging in marriage, a way in which human sexual energy can best fulfil its promise of enriching social life. For the Christian moralist there can be no going back on this. This is the achieved position from which we may now set out to explore the surrounding country and reconnoitre for any further advance.

To prepare for this reconnaissance we must look back over ground I have already covered and take stock of where we stand. If, varying the metaphor, we may be said to be standing on a platform, I have so far provided it with three planks.

1. In ethics, as in other fields of possible knowledge, God reveals his mind to men by inspiring them to grasp the significance of his creative and redemptive activity. His creative activity is revealed in the nature of the universe of his creation which is being made known to us through the insights of scientists, artists, historians and philosophers. This is an ongoing process in which fresh evidence or new insights often require revision of existing ideas. For the revelation of God's mind in the field of ethics the researches of psychologists, sociologists, moral philosophers, etc., are parallel to those of astronomers, geologists, etc., in the field of cosmology.

2. God's redemptive activity is revealed in the series of events which constitute the history of the Israelites, culminating in the coming of Christ and issuing in the history of the Christian church. These events provide fresh evidence which must be taken into account when we try to grasp the significance of God's creative activity as a whole. The significance of this evidence is itself subject to the necessity of being grasped through an ongoing process of revision in the light of fresh theological insights. Growth in understanding of God's revelation comes by a mutual exchange of insights between students of his creative and of his redemptive activity.

Two insights of outstanding importance for this Enquiry have come through the theological studies of this century.

(i) The New Testament Christians were not men who had a full understanding of what Christianity is to which we must get back. They were the men who, seeing things with the eyes of their time and place, took the first steps in trying to grasp the significance of the revelation of God in Christ, a process which has been going on ever since, in which we are still engaged.

(ii) From that revelation in Christ we learn that God is not concerned simply to save a number of human beings out of a perishing world. So far as this world is concerned his underlying purpose is the creation of a community of individualized free persons who will co-operate freely with him and with one another in caring and working for its welfare.[1] True religion is not concern for one's own salvation but for the accomplishment of this purpose. Penitence should spring from the discovery of how one's sinfulness gets in the way of this caring and working; the joyful acceptance of God's forgiveness, and the desire for growth in holiness, from the faith that in spite of it our heavenly Father continues to entrust us with our share in the family business. The church in the world is the continuing earthly body in and through which the risen ascended Lord is carrying on his work of rescuing and remaking creation in accordance with the Father's will. This was well expressed in an exposition of Christian worship given at a Roman Catholic eucharistic congress in Bombay :

We were there for participation in the eternal mysteries of God, to worship and to adore. . . . Being a Christian means involvement in the world of want and hunger, of technology and racial tension. The involvement springs from the living mystery of Jesus Christ at home among us. To be a Christian is to know that He, the source of light and life, is at the centre of life, one's own and the world's; and through worship to borrow the eyes of God with which to see and enter the modern world with all its possibilities for good or evil, and, with Christ, in Christ, to redeem it from within.[2]

Christian ethics today cannot be content to prescribe what

[1] Cp. my *For Faith and Freedom*, Vol. I, pp. 182ff.
[2] Quoted from the periodical *Frontier* (London, Spring 1965), p. 64.

should be required of those who are seeking to be saved; its task is to help men and women to learn how best to find and do the Father's will for the welfare of all his creatures.

3. In considering the history of Christian marriage we have seen how the element of romantic love and the right of women to equality of status have had to make good their claim to recognition. I am inclined to think that the two subjects are more closely interconnected than might appear at first sight, that without a right appreciation of the interests of women and of how things look from their point of view we shall not learn how to enable romantic love to make its best contribution. We may find some further light on this as we look out from marriage to the wider field of human sex relations in general.

Something more must be said about my second plank. We are familiar with the question of the relation between Christian ethics as concerned with the way in which professing Christians should behave and Christian ethics as claiming to reveal God's will for the behaviour of men and women in general. Traditionally the underlying assumption has been the importance of determining the grounds on which one may expect a favourable or unfavourable verdict on the Day of Judgment. What difference will it make to our thinking if Christ has taught us that we are to forget to be concerned about what happens to ourselves, to give our whole attention to sharing in his care for the welfare of his creation, resolve to regard salvation as a possible by-product of this devotion, and leave the issue in his hands?

We shall no longer think of God as having provided us with a list of rules and regulations which we are to keep if we hope to reach the end of our journey in the haven where we would be, still less with a list of permissible shipwrecks. We shall be able to think in terms of the general ethical considerations discussed in my first chapter, to see all human acts as responses to situations in which the moral quality of the agent and that of the act are relative to the ends pursued and to what the circumstances call for and permit.

The end to be pursued is the rescue of the world from all that prevents it from embodying and making manifest something of the glory and beauty of its Creator, the Creator whose character is revealed to us in Jesus Christ. What the circumstances call for and permit can only be discovered by examining what they actually are. These circumstances, it will be remembered, play their part in making an act the kind of act it is. They qualify both the condition of the agent and the material which he has to hand, both the strength of the drinker's head and the alcoholic content of his drink.[3] On the side of the agent, the nature of a man's faith, Christian or otherwise, will be one of the conditioning factors. It will affect the way in which he sees a situation and the relative value of different possible lines of action. He will have to consider them in the context of the customs and moral judgments which characterize the civilization of his time and place, asking, if he is a Christian, whether through them God is calling on him to revise in any way the convictions which are traditional among those who share his faith. It is in this spirit that we now turn to survey the wider scene.

II

As I have already said, I grew up in Christian circles in which it was taken for granted that monogamy with mutual fidelity of husband and wife was the normal standard expected by God, that among Christians bachelors and spinsters did not have 'affairs', that pre-marital, extra-marital, and non-marital sexual intercourse was not done or talked about. It was known, of course, that there were loose-living men, demi-mondaines and prostitutes, but they were, so to speak, outside thepale. The worldly-wise maxim that a young man must be

[3] See above, p. 14.

allowed to 'sow his wild oats' was not acceptable, and its extension to young women was unthinkable.[4] That would not be a true picture of the society in which we are living in England today, as it is known to us in the lives of ourselves and our friends and acquaintances, is represented in novels and plays and is unveiled by the researches of sociologists. So far from not being done or talked about, pre-marital, extra-marital and non-marital sexual intercourse is taken for granted as something which is nothing to be ashamed of, will probably have a place in any life that is worth living, and can be described in detail in books that are on sale for all the world to read.

To anyone brought up as I was it may appear at first sight as though there has been a breakdown in English standards of sexual morality, as though the men and women of today (especially the young men and young women) should be reproached for having abandoned ways of thinking and believing which earlier had been rightly approved. But more careful thought leads one to question this verdict on two grounds.

1. No doubt there is greater freedom in matters of sex than was customary sixty years ago. But this in itself is not necessarily proof of widespread moral laxity. There are indeed some advocates of sexual licence who are impatient of all restraint, and some journalists, playwrights and novelists who seem to accept them as voicing the authentic spirit of the age. But there is also evidence which goes to show that both approval and condemnation may be based on exaggerated estimates of the extent of moral laxity. I quote from a report on a piece of research which has been carried out in recent years under the auspices of the Central Council for Health Education:

It is hoped that those who are concerned about teenage sexual behaviour will be able to make use of some of the specific facts uncovered by this research. For example, it seems to be common practice to end a criticism of adolescent sexual

4 See above, p. 45; see further below, pp. 104ff.

behaviour by adding that we all know the bad ones are an exception, and that most of the youth of this country are a grand clean-living bunch of lads. But this qualification is as wrong as the criticism is inept. For the results of this research show clearly that those who are having sexual intercourse are not a tiny minority. In round figures something over 350,000 boys and girls under the age of twenty have had experience of pre-marital intercourse.

But although it is not a small minority, it is not a majority, and those who are concerned about this problem might begin by asking why, in view of the great strength of the sexual drive, there are not more teenagers who are sexually experienced. . . .

Despite the social and physiological pressures towards sexual intercourse, many teenagers manage to resist these influences. This research has found several differences between those who do and those who do not have sexual intercourse. . . . These differences do not reveal serious anti-social tendencies in those teenagers with experience of sexual intercourse. . . .

Nor is there any evidence that pre-marital sexual intercourse leads to or encourages adulterous relations after marriage. . . .

Those who are worried about the extent of pre-marital sexual intercourse among teenagers must accept that these activities cannot be eliminated altogether in the foreseeable future.[5]

Moreover, there is evidence that among a good many people, both old and young, the coming of the present freedom in thought and speech has brought a positive growth in moral seriousness. It has led to a questioning of conventionally accepted judgments, a refusal to be content with teaching that cannot make good its claim to be based on sound ethical principles. In so far as this questioning springs from the conviction

[5] M. Schofield, *The Sexual Behaviour of Young People* (London, 1965), p. 253.

that our traditional teaching about sex shows insufficient respect for human personality as a whole, it is to be welcomed.[6]

2. When we accuse the present age of having thrown overboard the moral standards of sixty years ago we assume that the morality of the circles in which I grew up was representative of the life of the country as a whole. It gives one a reassuring sense of proportion to read of English life in the eighteenth century as experienced by Henry Fielding in his work as magistrate and reformer of police and as described in James Boswell's *Journal* and John Cleland's *Fanny Hill*.[7] These give the impression that our morality in the eighteenth century was very much like what today is portrayed in newspapers, plays and novels. With one important exception, what is new in the so-called 'new morality' is not what is being done but the openness with which it is portrayed.

When we read other writings of that period, such novels, for example, as those of Fielding himself, of Defoe, Smollett, Richardson and Fanny Burney, we can see how the world of which they were writing was the world of Boswell and Cleland. But we have to 'read between the lines' to see it because such things could not be openly acknowledged in the polite society of the time. It looks to me as though the persistence of this convention, reinforced by prevailing tendencies in the Victorian age, succeeded in producing the outlook of the world in which I grew up, concealed from polite eyes what was actually going on all the time, and prevented it from receiving attention which we cannot withhold now that the veil has been stripped from our eyes.

[6] See, e.g., K. C. Barnes, *He and She* (Penguin Edition, 1964); E. Patey, *Young People Now* (London, 1964).

[7] See F. Homes Dudden, *Henry Fielding: His Life and Times* (Oxford, 1952), Vol. II, chs. xxvi, xxvii. To get the full flavour of *Fanny Hill* one must read the edition published in New York by G. P. Putnam's Sons, not the bowdlerized Sunday-school version issued by Mayflower-Dell in England.

It will be worth our while to consider first the factors which gave birth to this convention. There seem to have been at least the following three.

1. We have seen how deeply rooted in pre-Christian thought were emotional attitudes towards sex which regarded it as something demonic and terrifying, or as religiously defiling, or as deserving to be treated with reverence as sacred and private. New Testament Christianity brought the initial impetus which should lead to our rescue from the first two of these and the development of the third. But it takes the church a long time to grasp the full meaning of the revelation of God in Christ and the first two may still have had a powerful influence on the Christianity of eighteenth-century England.

2. Its literature was the literature of the elegant society in the class structure of that age. It was concerned with the doings of gentlefolk who lived in a world of their own. Economically they were dependent on the labours of their underlings, but the 'short and simple annals of the poor' were no worthy object of interest for the readers of polite literature. In that polite world for a girl or woman to lose her reputation for chastity was to lose her right to the sympathetic interest of her equals. The irregular sexual behaviour of men was enjoyed for the most part with companions from the unchronicled underworld.

3. The view of sex as essentially defiling was not the only inheritance from pre-Christian ideas which continued to infect Christian thought. There was also the widespread acceptance of male dominance in sexual relations, the treatment of the interests of girls and women as subservient to those of men. A man might be known to have a mistress without losing caste in the elegant society of the eighteenth century, a woman could not be known to be one. That this is no longer the case is the important exception to the similarity between the circumstances of that age and those of today.

What light does this comparison throw on the whole history of God's education of man in the ethics of sex, and of the part to be played in it by the revelation of God in Christ?[8]

We have noted the following features already existing in the world into which Christianity came not quite two thousand years ago.

(i) The universal prevalence of sexual attraction and the necessity of its regulation in the interests of civilized social life.

(ii) A variety of marriage customs instituted to meet this necessity of regulation.

(iii) The irrelevance of romantic love in consideration of the grounds on which marriages should be arranged. It would be absurd to think that what we call romantic love was never experienced or given expression in sexual intercourse. When it was, it might or might not be within marriage.

(iv) A general agreement that for men, at any rate, to have a life worth living sexual intercourse was a necessity for which provision must be made, apart from as well as within marriage.

(v) The general prevalence of male dominance in the sense that girls and women are treated as existing to serve the needs and interests of men.

The combination of these last three features involved the existence of women to meet the sexual needs of men unsatisfied by legally married wives. The social status of such women would depend on local custom and their own abilities.

I want to suggest the hypothesis that God has been, and still is, calling on the church to take these existing features in human behaviour and work them into a pattern which shall enable our sexual activity to make its best contribution to the enrichment of social life. We have begun by taking in hand the christianization of marriage. Here so far, under the guidance of the Holy Spirit, we have brought romantic love from its peripheral status into a central position, and have made some progress towards welcoming women into an equal partner-

[8] See above, pp. 25ff.

ship with men. For the first of these it was necessary that our way of loving should be transformed by learning from Christ 'how love might be, hath been indeed, and is'. To quote what I have written elsewhere : 'At our present stage in the creative process, the stage at which it is only fitfully and here and there that we can love like this, it is usually, if not always, through feelings rooted in the sexual character of our human nature. From the experience of what it is sometimes given to us to feel in connection with those to whom we are physically attracted we can form some idea of a world in which we could care for all men as now we care for him or her. It is from our experience of *eros* that we begin really to understand what is meant by *agape*.'[9]

We have still much to learn about the right way of recognizing the claims of women to equality in partnership. Meanwhile the christianization of marriage has to be wrought out in a world in which the fourth of the above features is still prevalent. That for men to live lives worth living they must have opportunities for sexual intercourse either within or outside marriage, and that there must be women to provide them is no new doctrine. It has been taken for granted from pre-Christian times right on through the eighteenth and nineteenth into the twentieth century. If there is anything new in the thought of today it is that to have lives worth living women must have it no less than men. It may be that the granting of this measure of equality to women will be found to have marked a turning-point in the christianization of sex relations in general.

As we look back over history it becomes clearer and clearer that the key to the problem lies in *men* discovering that sexual intercourse is not a necessity for a full and rich life on earth, that it is self-control in this respect that enables a man to explore the depths and heights of love. Instead of having learned this lesson and put it into practice men have expected those they marry to learn it for themselves and other women to give them what their wives do not.

But how were men to learn it? And how are they? We can no longer avoid looking squarely at the fact that the Christian religion has the cross at the heart of it. 'If any man would come after me, let him deny himself and take up his cross.' This is a truth which is not peculiar to our experience of sex. It may help us to see its bearing in this field if we consider it more widely.

In two passages in the Pauline Epistles loose living in matters of sex is coupled with avarice. The writer of Ephesians 4.17–5.21 speaks of people who give themselves up to lasciviousness, to work all uncleanness with covetousness, and says: 'But fornication, and all uncleanness or covetousness, let it not even be named among you.' The parallel is in I Thess. 4.3-6: 'This is the will of God, even your sanctification, that ye abstain from fornication, that each one of you know how to possess his own vessel in sanctification and honour, not in the passion of lust . . . that no man overreach and defraud his brother in business.'

From the point of view of Christian ethics this is an illuminating collocation of the worlds of sex and business. It suggests that in the Hellenistic cities of St Paul's time the centres of popular interest were very much the same as they are for us today, Wall Street and Times Square on one side of the Atlantic, the City and Piccadilly Circus on the other. And just as one is assured that it is unreasonable to expect a man to be sexually continent, so one is confidently told that it is impossible in these days to be a Christian in business.

Nine times out of ten when a man says that it is impossible to be a Christian in business he means by 'being a Christian' keeping certain prescribed rules in order to save his soul. There are times when he has to say or do things that are not strictly honest, and in his dealings with competitors or customers he cannot love his neighbours as himself. Hence he concludes that he must either give up his Christianity for his business, or come out of business and seek to support his wife and family in some philanthropic activity, or try to conceal from himself that he is living a life of dishonest compromise.

Here is a man in a situation which requires analysis by a kind of ethical thinking to which many business men are unaccustomed. He needs to be helped to see that there are three factors to be reckoned with.

(i) He is mistaken in thinking that being a Christian means being concerned with the state of his own soul or having a clear conscience. It means sharing in God's care for the goodness of his creation and the welfare of his creatures.

(ii) As often as not, in the present state of the world, we find ourselves in situations in which none of the courses open to us is wholly free from evil. Quite apart from business, for example, we may have to choose between telling a lie and breaking a confidence.[10] Since the character of acts is constituted by their circumstances, we have to ask which of those now open to us will best express our devotion to God's care for his creation. This, though it may involve telling the lie or breaking the confidence, will be the right thing for us to do. We cannot avoid the fact that we share in the life of a sinful world, and therefore the Christian must expect to have an uneasy rather than a clear conscience.

(iii) We live in an industrial and commercial civilization in which through developments due to scientific and technological research the conditions of human life are greatly improved. It is not always easy to remember that this application of the knowledge and skill that God is giving us is part of our share in his creative activity expressing his care for our welfare. Our traditional religious imagery is such that it is easy to think of a farmer as doing God's work when he is ploughing the fields and scattering or looking after his sheep; it is not so easy to see God at work in the activities of the industrial

10 See above, p. 15.

manager or shop steward, or of the insurance man through whom provision is made for their support in sickness and pension in old age. Yet the goods and services which these supply are simply an enlargement of the provision for our welfare made by the farmer's bread and beef and bacon, butter and eggs.

If the inefficient farmer is a bad workman for God, so too is the inefficient industrialist or business man. But they operate in a world in which there are various customs and conventions among the circumstances which determine the choices open to them. A manager's loyalty to his firm, or a workman's loyalty to his union, may be in conflict with the claims of truth-telling or neighbour-loving. At some moment, of course, the issue may be such that he rightly decides that he must stand up to his firm or union and risk the loss of his present means of livelihood. That may be the form of the cross he has to bear. But usually, day in and day out, it will take the form of trying to serve God and his fellow men as honestly and lovingly as may be possible in accordance with the customs and conventions of the industrial or business world. In these there is much that is deplorable, much that is in need of reform, much that will inevitably involve decisions that lie heavy on the Christian conscience. For him the bearing of the cross will be resistance to the temptation to give it all up for the sake of gaining a peace of mind which he mistakenly confuses with the salvation of his soul.

There is more to be learned from this comparison of sexual with industrial and business ethics. In both fields we are presented with material to be used in the service of God for the enrichment of human life. In both we are presented with opportunities to pursue our own personal gratification. There is a parallel between the way in which the efficient use of material resources and of sexual energy can enrich human living; and there is a parallel between the way in which, in both, we can be tempted to care more about our own satis-

faction than about God's will for the well-being of his creatures.[11] We may be thankful that both in business and in marriage success brings its rewards. It is good that efficiency in
business should be rewarded with affluence. It is good that,
both within and without marriage, the right regulation of
sexual activity should bring its own kind of happiness. But
both provide the circumstances in which we have to face the
fundamental challenge of Jesus Christ, the question whether
the mainspring of our life is to be self-seeking or self-giving.[12]
Lovers and business men, like artists, scientists and scholars,
have to learn that the secret of truly successful living is to do
what is done because it is worth doing in itself and not for the
sake of the reward. St Paul was surely right in treating the
pursuit of wealth and sex as the two fields in which men have
most need to learn how to control their desires.

In the world at large it is commonly assumed that men must
be allowed to have experience of sexual intercourse in order
to have lives worth living. Women are making good their
claim that the goose must be allowed the same sauce as the
gander. Meanwhile the Christian church goes on maintaining
that both men and women should deny themselves this experience, except in so far as they bind themselves to one
another in lifelong monogamous marriage. How can this re-
striction be accepted as either reasonable in itself or designed
for the enrichment of human living?

As I have already said, it is not a question of what should
be required of those who are seeking to be saved, but of
helping men and women how best to find and do God's work
for the welfare of his creatures.

It seems to me that in respect of both wealth and sex the
coming of Jesus Christ initiated a movement aiming at enab-

[11] Cp. I Tim. 6.7-19.
[12] I call this the fundamental challenge because our difficulty in
grasping our Lord's teaching that true religion is concern for the welfare of God's creation and not concern for our own salvation shows how
deeply is self-seeking ingrained in our human nature.

ling men to gain control of their activities in accordance with God's will. In neither field have we as yet achieved full mastery. This is not surprising in view of the conditions in which the task had to be begun. God's will to create men and women as genuinely free finite persons required their redemption to be by way of winning their free co-operation in it. For this co-operation to be effective men needed three things : (i) to be brought to share God's vision of what was aimed at; (ii) to be cleansed from their own sinfulness which kept them from seeing and working for it; (iii) to be given the power to control themselves and their circumstances that was necessary for its achievement.

It is the first and third of these with which we are now concerned, the sharing of the vision and the receipt of power to achieve it.[18] In the experimental verification of the Christian hypothesis the two have to walk hand in glove. It is only as we receive power to live by it that we come to see more clearly what the vision is and discover that it is a vision of a life worth living.

In the circles in which I grew up we may have been blindly ignorant of how life was being lived in the world around us, of what it had to offer in the way of sexual experience and of what we were missing. We may, too, have been unaware of the extent of the suffering caused by narrow-minded puritanism. Here on earth we can none of us have all possible experiences, as Darwin learned when he had to give up his musical pursuits in the interest of his scientific research. How far we were helped by our narrowness of outlook I cannot say; we certainly did have the experience of discovering that it is possible for a man to live by the then accepted standards of Christian sexual behaviour without psychological disaster or sense of impoverishment of life. Indeed many of us would

[18] For the second see my *The Bible and the Training of the Clergy* (London, 1963), pp. 89ff., and *The Doctrine of the Atonement* (London, 1951), *passim*.

maintain that through this discipline our lives, so far from being impoverished, were enriched. It enabled us to discover for ourselves something more of 'how love, might be, hath been indeed, and is', love in which our sexual urges come to their true and most fruitful fulfilment.

In his *Moral Adventure*[14] B. H. Streeter instances the way in which the door is opened to partnership in joint enterprises for men and women when any question of sexual intercourse is ruled out by common consent. We need not be so heavily serious as to confine this to professional co-operation, as in medicine, law, or the work of the church. In our social and recreational life, for both men and women, there is a quality in the companionship and friendship of members of the other sex which gives it a colour and a richness that is all its own. It is rooted in our sexual feelings and may be frankly acknowledged and enjoyed as such. It can be most fully and frankly acknowledged and enjoyed when it is agreed on both sides that to go to bed together is not the only way in which their mutual attraction can most fruitfully enrich their lives. It is in this way that a general acceptance of the Christian discipline can assist in eliminating the poison of jealousy from the system of Christian marriage.[15] It is a way of life which can produce such lovers an Anthony Trollope's Roger Carbury.[16]

Hitherto I have mainly emphasized the negative element in this way of life, its hiding from our eyes the truth about how in general life is lived in the world we live in. To redress the balance I am now stressing the positive contribution it has made to our understanding of the possibilities of human

[14] London, 1928.

[15] See above, pp. 6off.

[16] *The Way We Live Now*, chapters lxvi, xciii, c. Trollope, incidentally, was in advance of his time in his sensitive understanding of the woman's point of view. A contemporary review of *The Vicar of Bullhampton* in *Vanity Fair* treated the dispute between the vicar and dissenters as the main theme of the book and dismissed Mary Lowther as a tiresome girl who caused a good man unnecessary trouble by not knowing her own mind.

achievement. The kind of continence that once it was thought could only be expected of certain peculiar 'holy men' has come to be accepted among Christians as the standard of behaviour for men in general, for laymen as well as clergy. In the total population of the world Christians are a minority. But it is a minority big enough for them to be able to claim a hearing for the standards they believe they ought to uphold. A young Englishman who served on the lower deck in the navy from 1943 to 1946 once told me that two things struck him in the sexual behaviour of his messmates in foreign ports: one was the way in which as a matter of course the unmarried would consort with available girls and women, the other was the extent to which the married held themselves to be under obligation to be faithful to their wives at home. No doubt there were exceptions in both classes. If this observation were true, the proportion of faithful husbands and continent bachelors would illustrate the measure of the church's success in the experimental verification of its hypothesis.

How have we come this far? We are tempted to think that from the start this has been the Christian sex ethic, that this is how the New Testament Christians thought and lived, that from that day to this it has been the standard theory and practice of the church. But this would be to surrender to what I have called the negative side of the outlook of the Christian circles in which I grew up, an outlook which not only blinded us to facts of contemporary life but made us unhistorical in our reading back into New Testament Judaism and Christianity our own ideas of how we should think and live.[17] When we try to study the biblical evidence in the context of the sociological study of human sex activity in general, we have to take a new look at what St Paul had to say on the subject of fornication. We cannot think of him as having written for a Christian community which had our present-day ideas and outlook. It was one in which it was generally taken for granted that

[17] See above, pp. 44ff.

society must have a place for women who would provide for men's sexual needs outside marriage; in which men could not be expected to do without them; in which neither Jews nor Christians need necessarily be monogamous.

St Paul, then, was not writing in the kind of circumstances which have led a present-day bishop to say 'fornication is always wrong'. He was writing for Christians among whom, for men at any rate, it was accepted as a matter of course. In the instance which called forth his stern denunciation it was due to the particular nature of the offence (I Cor. 5.1-8). Nevertheless, he was not happy about it all. He goes on to say that both in their sex life and in their business life the church should expect of its members the kind of standards which for us today are still the ideal.

Let us try to put ourselves in his position and see the situation with his eyes. Although he was ministering to a mixed congregation of Jewish and gentile Christians who saw nothing necessarily wrong in fornication as such, he knew that there was widespread respect for the holiness of men who were known to abstain from sexual intercourse on religious grounds, grounds which might be due to Jewish or Christian or pagan beliefs. Let us suppose that he shared this respect and reverence, that for him the lives of such men gave evidence that the grace of God was sufficient to enable men to be able to live them, and that his ideal for the Christian community was that all its members should come to share in this mastery of spirit over flesh. His argument in I Cor. 6.12-20 was not a rebuke to rebels against or backsliders from generally accepted Christian standards; it was an attempt to give reasonable grounds for urging the church to adopt new ones, for the kind of discipline he had just proposed in the last five verses of the previous chapter.

This understanding of the situation throws light on the succeeding passage in which occur the well-known verses : 'I say to the unmarried and to widows, it is good for them if they abide even as I. But if they have not continency, let them marry. It is better to marry than to burn.' It is objected that in these verses St Paul endorses a low view of marriage as existing to satisfy the desires of the flesh, and implies a low view of women as existing to satisfy the desires of men. These objections are valid only on the assumption that he must be held to have said the last word on the subject. When we take them as directed to the actual situation, they show him to have been a realist, recognizing the existing customs and conventions and enlisting them in the service of his ideal.

As we have already seen, Ephesians comes from the same sociological conditions and contains the beginning of the redemption of marriage, and indeed of all human sex relations, from bondage to evil. So long as a man is thinking of girls and women in general it is natural that their role as potential partners in sexual enjoyment should be dominant in his thoughts and feelings. But when he comes to love, and love deeply, a particular woman for herself, when his sexual imagination is harnessed to thoughts of *her*, there is a change. *She* cannot be thought of as existing for his own satisfaction. She is to be loved as a whole person. His desire for sexual union with her is merged in a desire to share his whole life with her, to find his own satisfaction in the joy of giving himself to increase her joy. He becomes sensitive to her thoughts and feelings in a way which has a new influence on his own. To be married to her will not be a concessionary licence to self-indulgence. On the contrary. It will lead him to discover in himself a new power of self-control. There will be occasions when he is conscious that his wife is not at the time disposed for intercourse or even for any close physical contact, occasions on which he himself is fiercely burning with desire, when self-restraint will not be a negative act of repression but the positive expression of his love, the proof of its reality and its depth. As he learns this lesson with the help of some one particular woman, it will transform his way of thinking about all women. He will come to see them, too, as whole persons, as equals whose companionship is to be sought and enjoyed on the basis of common interests in a variety of fields of which mutual sexual attraction is only one. It is an important one, and one which can contribute much to the enjoyment, but one which needs to be disciplined if it is to give of its best.

We cannot claim that love of this kind is a plant that can only grow on Christian soil, if by that we mean on the ground of conscious Christian faith. As Father, Son and Spirit God is at work throughout the whole world. All we can say is that wherever men discover what it is to love like this, whether they be Christians or men of some other faith or of none, we recognize it as loving after the manner of the love of Christ for his church.

'It is better to marry than to burn.' When we ask how God is using the Bible to speak to us today we do not read this commendation of marriage as a concessionary licence to self-indulgence but as an instrument for helping us to grow in self-knowledge and self-control. How far St Paul could have foreseen these consequences of his teaching it is impossible to say. It may be that it needed the growing experience of the church to bring out the meaning of his words. Here we have to reckon with the effect of the coming of monasticism. Again, as in the case of St Paul and other biblical writers, we have to distinguish between what they thought at the time and what God intended to reveal through their teaching and actions. It may be that the inclusion of the vow of chastity in the threefold monastic rule was based on a mistaken view of sex; it may be that there was a dark side to its enforcement which led to instances of hypocrisy, scandal and mental catastrophe. But the fact remains that the monastic movement was a demonstration of the possibility of masculine continence on a large enough scale to show that St Paul's ideal of its becoming the rule for Christians in general was not an idle dream. This view receives support from the fact that the vow is reproduced in the Rule of Taizé community as explained by Prior Schutz in *Vivre l'Aujourd'hui de Dieu*.[18]

The Christian church, then, is engaged in the experimental verification of the hypothesis that the way to enable sex most fruitfully to enrich human life will be by the exercise of the kind of self-discipline that I have tried to describe. We have reached the stage at which the actual choice before us lies between accepting whatever it may cost to persevere in the experiment and acquiescing in the view of sex portrayed in such books as James Baldwin's *Another Country* and Nell Dunn's *Up the Junction*. Corporately the church needs to say of itself what St Paul said of himself:

'I press on, hoping to take hold of that for which Christ once took hold of me. . . . I do not reckon myself to have got hold of it yet. All I can say is this: forgetting what is behind me, and reaching out for that which lies ahead, I press towards the goal to win the prize which is God's call to the life above, in Christ Jesus.'[19]

III

I have said that in order to take part in and set forward this experiment men need three things: to be won to see what it is aiming at and to agree that the goal is worth striving for; to be cleansed from whatever in themselves prevents them from joining in; to be given the power to control themselves and their circumstances which is necessary for its achievement.[20] The church is not to think of itself as the ark in which it is to gather those who seek to be saved out of the perishing world, but as existing to serve the world by the provision of these three requirements through its ministry of word and sacraments. But before going on to consider in more detail what this will involve, we must briefly notice one further service which is, perhaps, the most fundamental of all.

[18] Taizé, 1959, pp. 97ff.
[19] Phil. 3.14 (NEB).   [20] See above, p. 92.

'As the Father hath sent me, even so send I you.' The church is commissioned to carry on the *incarnate* ministry of its Lord. 'Not to judge but to save.' Judging in the sense of pronouncing judgment on what is done is not for the church militant here on earth. 'In the world that is to be, when the Son of Man is seated on his throne in heavenly splendour, you my followers will have thrones of your own where you will sit as judges.' In the New Testament records of the first attempts of Christians to grasp the significance of Christ's saving ministry there are two mysterious verses which we cannot ignore. 'Who his own self bare our sins in his body upon the tree.' 'Him who knew no sin he made to become sin on our behalf: that we might become the righteousness of God in him.'[21]

'Who his own self bare our sins in his body on the tree.' All attempts at expounding the doctrine of the atonement are attempts to unpack and exhibit the hidden contents of this phrase. That is not the subject of this book. But it is relevant to say that in whatever sense we think of Jesus Christ having borne our sins on the cross, and of God having made him to be sin on our behalf, in that same sense we must think of God having called the church into existence to bear the sins of the world and to be sin on the world's behalf. The church is the earthly body in which the Lamb of God is continuing his work of taking away the sins of the world.

In my book on the atonement I have said what I can about ways in which the church can play its part in bearing and taking away. What about being 'made sin'? Here I cannot hope to do more than touch the surface of a deep mystery. I can perhaps best approach it by asking what we mean in our

[21] John 20.21; 12.47; Matt. 19.28; I Pet. 2.24; II Cor. 5.21. The last two are quoted from the Revised Version of 1881. Here the New English Bible, determined (as so often) to save its readers from the trouble of trying to think what the writers of difficult passages may have meant, gives a suggested interpretation instead of a translation of what they wrote.

worship when we say the general confession. There have been many times when I have been troubled by the question whether there is not an element of hypocrisy involved in our use of its apparently exaggerated language. I now see that the question arose from accepting the idea of the church as the sphere within which its members should be concerned with seeking their own salvation, confessing their own personal sins with a view to their own personal spiritual cleanliness. But when one thinks of the church as called by God to be 'made sin' for the world, to accept responsibility for the world's need of cleansing, the case is altered. There is neither exaggeration nor hypocrisy when on reading such a book as Julius Horwitz's *The Inhabitants*[22] one joins in saying

'We have erred and strayed from thy ways like lost sheep. We have followed too much the devices and desires of our own hearts. We have offended against thy holy laws. We have left undone those things which we ought to have done; and we have done those things which we ought not to have done; and there is no health in us.'

What the church has to offer to the world in matters of sex is not a judgment on its habits pronounced by those who have been saved out of it to enjoy the peace of keeping their consciences clear and know all the answers. It is such counsel and advice as we may be able to give to the extent that God the Holy Spirit opens our eyes to see the implications of the revelation in Christ, helps us to try to live by it, and enables us to understand its relevance in the circumstances of our time.

[22] Penguin Edition, 1965.

6

THE CURE OF SOULS

I

THE CURE OF SOULS. This fine old phrase is quoted in the Oxford English Dictionary from writings as early as 1340 and 1490. It is defined as 'the spiritual charge or oversight of parishioners and lay people; the office or function of a curate'.

If an ethic be a statement of rules or principles intended to be normative for the conduct of all sorts and conditions of men in all sorts of times and places, we are not yet in a position to state what is *the* Christian ethic relative to any department of life, including sex. 'Christ gave his life; it is for Christians to discern the doctrine.' We are engaged in this work of discernment. As the years go by the Holy Spirit uses the experience of men and women in different ages and cultures to open our eyes to a fuller understanding of the revelation of God in Christ. Not until the end of time will it be possible to stand up on platform or in pulpit and give a detailed exposition of Christian sex ethics.

This understanding of God's self-revelation as a continuing educational process explains why the Christian life in all ages appears to consist of 'an unceasing dialogue and tension between rule-agapism and act-agapism'.[1] We have to be true to what we have already learned. As Bernard Bosanquet put it: 'How can there be progress if no definite ground is ever to be recognized as gained? There is no progress in a Penelope's

---

[1] Paul Ramsey, *Deeds and Rules in Christian Ethics* (Edinburgh and London, 1965), p. 24.

web.'[2] Thus I have spoken of Christianity having initiated 'a way of thinking about and engaging in marriage, a way in which human sexual energy can best fulfil its promise of enriching social life', and have said that 'for the Christian moralist there can be no going back on this'.[3] But we are still far from knowing all that is involved in it for ourselves, and from being able to commend what we have learned to others and to share it with them. We must persevere in exploring its possibilities, trusting that God will use the tension between the lessons of the past and the experiences of the present to open our eyes to a fuller understanding of his will for men and women.

Meanwhile in each age and place we clergy have to do our best to perform 'the office or function of a curate', to try to help those who come to us for spiritual counsel and advice.

For this our Enquiry provides four guiding considerations.

1. We are clergy of a church called into existence by God to be the body through which he can express his care for the welfare of his creatures and bear whatever it may cost to take away the sins of the world. Our spiritual counsel will not be directed towards advising men how to secure their own salvation but towards helping them to see how best to play their part in this caring and bearing. In the attempt to do this they will discover their own need of God's grace and be led by the Holy Spirit to growth in holiness, in which we should be able to help them further.

2. We are likely to be consulted not only by believing and practising Christians but also by others, some on the fringe of belief and others beyond it. To whatever group they belong we must try to help them *where they are*.

3. We must do our best to make our counsel and advice relevant to the circumstances of today, remembering how minds are influenced by the pressures of the contemporary

---

[2] *The Principle of Individuality and Value* (London, 1912), p. vi.
[3] See above, p. 78.

social climate of opinion on sexual questions. Simply to dismiss all sexual intercourse outside marriage will be of no use to those who are aware that both inside and outside there are moral distinctions of better and worse and want to be helped to discriminate.

4. In so far as the insights which have come to us through the revelation of God in Christ are moral insights they belong to a sphere in which (i) an act can only be intelligibly defined as a response to a situation; (ii) the circumstances of the situation enter into the making of the act the kind of act it is; and (iii) situations may be such that none of the possible choices can be called unequivocally good. I have suggested that the words 'right' and 'wrong' should be used for what ought or ought not to be done in a particular situation, so that an act which is not 'good' may nevertheless be 'right'.[4] This is why I could not myself make such a generalized statement as that 'fornication is always wrong'.

Two instances may help to expose some of the difficulties of the problem.

In 1914 a young Englishman was in Germany when war was declared on August 4th. He was promptly rounded up and interned in a prison camp for enemy aliens. His knowledge of language and habits was such as to enable him to pass as a German and he decided that it was his duty, if possible, to escape, make his way home, and enlist in the service of his own country. The escape was successful, but the nearest frontier was a long way off, and the only place where he could spend a night without risk of discovery was a brothel. The conflict arose, to use Hartmann's phrase, 'from the structure of the situation': he had to violate either his duty to his country or concern for his own chastity.

Some years ago I met a youngish widow who, after a disastrous marriage and miserable married life, was earning her own living. She had fallen in love with a man who was work-

---

[4] See above, p. 16.

ing in the same office. He was a married man with a wife and two children and she had become his mistress. She said she knew and liked his wife and children and would take care to avoid doing anything which might spoil or break up his marriage; indeed she claimed quite sincerely that what she was able to give her lover enabled him to be a better husband and father. I told her that I did not like the situation, that sooner or later the time might come when the man would find it impossible to go on living a double life and that one or other of his two women would have to pay the cost. She said that it should certainly not be the wife and that for herself, having faced the risk, she was prepared to take it. When I asked on what grounds she could have made such a foolish decision she replied, quite simply and quietly, 'Because I love him'.

I remember feeling that that quietly spoken considered acceptance of utter risk was the expression of a quality of love more Christlike than anything of which I knew myself to be capable. She was not a member of the Church of England, and was no parishioner of mine. But I could not help asking myself : 'Supposing that she had been, and had come to tell me that for perseverance in her service of her lover and his family she needed the help of our Lord in the sacrament of Holy Communion, could I have turned her away?'

I have spoken of a Christlike quality of love. The phrase needs further attention, a fact that is curiously overlooked in many discussions of Christian sex ethics. In *Honest to God*, for example, the Bishop of Woolwich says that 'in the man Christ Jesus stands revealed . . . the depth and ground of all our being as Love'; and suggests that for our moral guidance it should be enough to know that 'if we have the heart of the matter in us, if our eye is single, then love will find out the way'. Apart from speaking of Jesus as 'the man for others and the man for God' and of 'self-giving love' he apparently assumes that his readers will understand what is meant by the 'love' which will find out the way. In his *Deeds and Rules in*

Christian Ethics Dr Paul Ramsey is content to speak of *agape* and *agapism* as though the transliteration of the Greek word will be sufficient to explain the kind of love that is meant.

At the other extreme is the modern use of the word 'love' to mean bodily sexual intimacy and intercourse. I say 'modern' because sixty years ago in English polite society and literature to say that a man and a woman were lovers or that he made love to her would not have meant what the words do in the novels of today. 'Harald and I have been lovers quite a time.' 'Polly sometimes wondered whether she would have let Gus come up to her room and make love to her if he had told her. . . .'[5]

Here are two distinct and different meanings of the word 'love', used in different circles of discourse in each of which it is assumed to be self-explanatory. Is it a matter of 'East is east and west is west and never the twain shall meet'? Or is there some connection between them and, if so, what? This question is surely vital to any enquiry into Christian sex ethics. I have never yet come across any discussion of it that has seemed to me satisfactory. I must try to start one on my own, but I cannot hope to do more than open the question up.

We will start from a middle point between the two extremes, midway between Dr Robinson's idea of the Love which is revealed to us in the man Christ Jesus as constituting the ground and depth of our being, and the thought of those for whom love is essentially the desire for and possible achievement of bodily sexual intercourse. At this middle point we are only thinking of human love, and human love at its best is assumed to be the mutual devotion of whole persons, body, soul and spirit, or feeling, thought and action, all three. Love will not be at its best if it is deficient in any of these. I take this as the starting-point because it is a point of view which can be shared by men of any religious faith or none.

Divergence towards the two extremes comes as a result of

[5] Mary McCarthy, *The Group* (Penguin Edition, 1966), pp. 124, 236.

emphasizing one or other of the elements in this complex whole. Emphasis on the bodily element of feeling leads naturally to the love of Norine and Harald, of Polly and Gus. Emphasis on harmony in mind and spirit may go so far as to obscure the importance of bodily attraction. I have already spoken of how far for a man and woman who have fallen in love with one another 'the pursuit of common interests may absorb the attention while their rootage is to all intents ignored or forgotten'.[6] But though it may be ignored or forgotten, it is still there. This is the fact that is overlooked by those who would set *eros* and *agape* over against each other and keep them as separate as east and west.

Whether we are dealing with relations between men and women, or between persons of the same sex, there is a special enrichment of friendship which has its roots in their bodily sexual attraction for each other. They may be quite unaware of where it comes from. All that a man or a woman may know is that to be with some people gives them a kind of enjoyment that they do not have with others, that a walk, a talk, a game, a journey or anything else done together with X would be a bore, but with Y would be a delight. It may never lead them to any acts of bodily endearment. They may be quite unable to give any intelligible account of just what kind of enjoyment it gives, or why it should be so. All this, it seems to me, becomes intelligible when we think of it as coming from physical sexual attraction down in the depths of our human being, sometimes mutual, sometimes unreciprocated. The reason why neither they nor we can be more explicit about the kind of enjoyment it gives is that the colouring it gives to life is, *sui generis*, unique, and cannot be described in terms of anything else.

Now let us go back to the beginning and think about how it comes to be. As growing boys and girls pass through adolescence into puberty they begin to feel this new kind of liking for one another. They may or may not have any awareness of its sexual origin. This will largely depend on the level of sophistication in the circles in which they have grown up. Such awareness is probably more widespread today than it was when I was a boy. Essentially in themselves these feelings are ambivalent, that is to say they can generate desire for physical intimacy and for mental and spiritual companionship, either or both. Here again in different individuals the proportionate strength of this or that kind of desire will largely be due to the ethical and cultural climate of opinion from which they come.

We must take care not to underestimate the capacity for truly generous love which these feelings can generate in the young. A recently published novel describes its opening scene as follows: 'The restaurant was dark, one of those . . . "romantic" places where debs go with their boy friends and dirty old men go with their girl friends and the lights are so low you can hardly see.'[7] Contemplating this scene a middle-aged moralist will know in himself what and how those old men are thinking and feeling and be in danger of reading those thoughts and feelings back into the minds of their juniors. In some cases it may be so. But to assume that in general they are looking forward to an evening's sexual delights for which the dinner is a prelude would be both unjust and untrue. A young man is just as likely to be thinking of how he can lay down his life at the feet of his beloved and find his own happiness in giving up the world for her. And it may be that they are discussing together their plans for rescuing the world from the mess their parents have made of it.

One and the same physiological affinity can and does generate these diverse patterns of thought and feeling. Our aim should be to encourage the growth of its power to fertilize and enrich all kinds of personal interest in the various activities that go to make life worth living. In some cases this en-

[7] Brian Glanville, *A Second Home* (London, 1965), p. 5.

richment will be enhanced by the enjoyment of physical sexual intercourse; in others the sexual element may continue to play its part below the level of conscious attention. The point I want to make is that for us human beings it is through our experience of sex that we can learn to know what it feels like to care for someone else in a way that can rightly be called love. Then it can be trained in such a way that we can extend this kind of caring beyond the circle of those with whom we have this kind of affinity. It is through the experience of *eros* that we learn what it feels like to love with *agape*.

God's education of man in the art of loving is of a piece with the method of his creative activity in general. In the evolutionary process we see some creatures rising to acquire new characteristics and powers as they adjust themselves to the conditions of fresh environments. In the eyes of a Christian believer they are receiving gifts from God as he takes them to share more fully in the reality he is creating.[8] Others remain content to be adapted to the environment from which they spring and get no further. Similarly we start our love life as creatures attracted to one another by physiological affinities which may be called by such names as *eros* or the mating urge. Through our experience of this we can learn to know something of that 'self-giving love' which for Dr Robinson is characteristic of God who is 'the depth and ground of all our being'. Here again we are receiving a gift from our Creator as he draws us on to share more fully in the reality which he is creating, the reality which is to consist of a community of genuinely free persons bound to himself and to one another in bonds of mutual personal love. It is in this context that we can speak of a Christlike quality of love.

We clergy and those for whom we are trying to perform the office or function of a curate are fellow pupils in God's school for education in the reality of love. As in all schools

[8] On this see my *For Faith and Freedom*, Vol. I, pp. 154, 163, 221; Vol. II, p. 107.

(i) education involves discipline and discipline only becomes effective in so far as it is accepted as self-discipline; and (ii) what can be taught and learned is conditioned by the climates of opinion in the homes and social circles from which the pupils come and in which they live.

(i) Our survey of Christian history has led to the conviction that the discipline to be aimed at is that involved in confining sexual intercourse to lifelong monogamous marriage based on and expressing the mutual love of equal partners.

(ii) We are all of us, clergy and laity alike, subject to the pressures on us of contemporary habits of thought and action. As I have already suggested, our situation may be more like that of Pastor Jean Gotto among the polygamists of Cameroun, or of St Paul in Corinth, than is often realized in what Prior Schutz calls our Christian ghettoes. Here in England the law would not allow a man to have more than one wife, but he might have one or more mistresses as well. Would such a man turn to us for counsel and advice? If not, why not? If he did, what should we have to say?

II

We will begin by considering how we may try to help men and women who are believing and practising Christians.

There is a traditional distinction in logic between the orders of being, of expounding and of learning. Logically the order of being may come first, but in the order of learning it is the goal of the quest and may be the last to be reached. The expositor stands in the middle. So far in this Enquiry we have been following the order of the learner, trying to discover for ourselves what is the truth of the matter. Now we pass to that of the expositor and have to consider how what we have learned can best be presented to men and women who are at different stages in the process of learning. The first necessity is to be clear in our own minds about what we have to present and it may help if, at the risk of repetition, I tabulate under seven heads the main points that seem to me to have emerged.

1. God's method of revelation in his creative and redemptive activity by doing things and inspiring men to grow in understanding the nature and significance of what he does.

2. The church as the fellowship of forgiven sinners through whom the risen Lord is carrying on his incarnate work for the welfare of the Father's world.

3. Church membership as enlistment to share in Christ's care for the Father's world and to be willing to bear whatever it may cost to set forward its welfare.

4. Ethics as concerned with acts which are responses to situations so that circumstances enter into the making of them the kind of acts they are.

5. Sex as ambivalent in its power to generate enjoyment both in physical intimacy and in mental and spiritual companionship.

6. Christian marriage as a contribution towards solving the problem of regulating human sexual activity in the interests of social welfare.

7. This contribution made possible by the power of the risen Christ at work in the lives of men and women.

I have said something, in the last chapter, of the self-discipline and self-control required of men and women if they are to play their part in the experimental verification of the Christian hypothesis. God calls us to share in both his creative and his redemptive activity. In St Paul's words we are to fill up on our part that which is lacking of the afflictions of Christ in our flesh for his body's sake which is the church.[9]

We must be quite clear that this self-discipline is called for in order that we may contribute towards making the best possible use of sex in human society. It is the positive, not the negative, side that needs to be stressed. Sex is not to be avoided as something nasty, shrunk from as something to be afraid of,

[9] Col. 1.24.

or renounced as a defilement to holiness. On the contrary it is a gift of God who rejoices when he sees his sons and daughters enjoying it to the full. But its misuse can lead to degradation and misery. It is to save it from this that it needs to be disciplined.

If we are to be able to help a believing and practising Christian we must be prepared to start with him *where he is*. If I find that he is with me in all that I have been trying to say in this book, as summarized under the above seven headings, there are some questions that will not need to be discussed. Of certain infractions of discipline he will no more ask 'Why shouldn't I?' than would an athlete in training or a soldier on active service. What he will need is encouragement to persevere and reminding of the importance of that 'habitual recollection' of which Martin Thornton writes in *The Rock and the River*.[10] And he may need help towards having a truly understanding sympathy with those who do not share his faith. 'The trouble with the Christians is not that they have strict morals, but that they don't seem to care very much. They don't care about the agonies of unhappy marriage, about the loneliness of the unmarried, about the dilemmas of the homosexual.'[11]

But there are believing and practising Christians who by no means believe in all that I have been led to hold under my seven headings. There are some who would think otherwise about God's method of revelation and about the nature and work of the church. There are some who would not be prepared to allow for the element of truth contained in situational ethics. There are some who cannot believe that sex is given to us by God to be enjoyed, or think of Christian marriage as a comparative novelty in human history which has still to win its way to acceptance as God's will for all his people. Some,

[10] London, 1965.
[11] Monica Furlong, reviewing books in *The New Christian* for February 10th, 1966, p. 20.

on the other hand, may be so sure of the value of sex as a
God-given enrichment of human life that they cannot believe
him really to require the discipline of lifelong monogamous
fidelity. Some will be unhappily married. Some, either married
or unmarried, will be enjoying sexual intercourse with partners who may themselves be either unmarried or other people's
husbands or wives. Some will be homosexual.[12] Any or all of
these may be more or less believing and practising Christians.
I say 'more or less' because there are infinite gradations in both
belief and practice, from those who have an intelligent grasp
of the Christian faith and are regular communicant members
of a church to those who are confusedly uncertain about what
they believe and happy-go-lucky in respect of both private
prayers and public worship.

What we have to do is try to listen with understanding
sympathy to what we are told and be prepared to start with
each person *at the point which he or she has reached* in the
order of learning.

It would be absurd to try to catalogue and discuss all the
various situations in which we may be called upon for counsel
and advice. From those of which I have heard I will select one
as an example of the kind of situations that have to be met.

An able mature woman filled with distinction an important
post in the educational world. She was prevented from marry-
ing by having to support and care for an aging mother. Unknown to the world she had for some years enjoyed a sexual
relationship with a man friend which not only enriched both
their lives but was also, she believed, the secret of the poise,
balance and graciousness which were of great value both in
her work and in her home life. She was also a devout Christian, a regular communicant, and drew from this the strength
to persevere in her service of the community and of her aging
parent. Not unnaturally she was uncomfortable in her mind
about this double life which was, to say the least, unconven-

[12] On this see B. Magee, *One in Twenty* (London, 1966).

tional and, if they knew about it, was likely to be disapproved by many, if not most, of her fellow Christians. So she consulted a priest. He listened and talked sympathetically, but in the end told her firmly that if she wished to continue as a communicant the association with her lover must stop. Unable to agree, she sought a second opinion from another priest who took a different line. As a result of his studies in psychology he accepted as true her belief that it was the sexual relationship which enabled her to be what she was in her work and at home. I don't know whether he had ever read Hartmann, but he recognized that her difficulty was due to what Hartmann would call the 'structure of the situation'.[13] She was in a situation similar to that of a man who has to choose between telling a lie and breaking a confidence and may have to decide that to tell the lie is the right thing to do. It would be wrong for her to cut herself off from either of the two sources of what gave value to her service of God in the world. It was unfortunate that her sexual relationship had to be extra-marital, but it could be that she would be right to continue it in the same way that it could be right for the man to tell his lie. If so, she must put her trust in God's full understanding of the whole situation, accept the enriching and helpful love as his gift, include it in her thanksgiving to him for all his goodness, and in her offering to him of her whole self, soul and body, for his service. With this, too, she must accept the inconveniences of continued secrecy and in all probability the persistence of an uneasy conscience. These will be part of the price she has to pay if she is to join in the church's filling up of the afflictions of Christ.

From what I have learned in the course of this Enquiry it seems to me that this second opinion is the right one. It gives a further illustration of the parallel between sexual and business ethics.[14] In both, the minds of men and women are conditioned by the contemporary climate of opinion, and their

[13] See above, p. 15.   [14] See above, pp. 88ff.

choices are restricted to those open to them in the circumstances in which they have to make their decisions. In so far as this second opinion involved a revision of traditional teaching expressed in the first it may have been an instance of God giving us new insight through psychological research.[15] What he had learned in that field enabled the priest to start with the two lovers where they were.

I have no idea how far advanced they were in understanding what God is teaching us of the place of the church in the world, or of his call to its members to help in the experimental verification of its sexual ethic. They may have been little aware of the grounds for the self-discipline required of those who hear and respond to this call which this Enquiry has brought to light.

The choices open to the priest were equally restricted by the circumstances of the case. He could take the traditional line and insist on his consultant renouncing either her association with her lover or her full church membership. Or he could decide, in spite of tradition, to give the advice he did. In either case he would be taking a risk. Insistence on immediate conformity to traditional discipline might result in complete severance of church membership. To set it aside might weaken the church's stand for its principles. To my mind this latter risk was the right one to take. Not only, as I have tried to show, was it based on a sound appreciation of God's method of revelation in the field of ethics, but it also held out the greater hope of strengthening in the long run the church's advocacy of monogamy. Within the fellowship of the church the couple might grow in their understanding of its vocation until they came to accept for themselves a discipline which they would reject when imposed by another on grounds they could not comprehend.

[15] See above, p. 78.

III

In my attempted analysis of the origin and development of human affection I have spoken of the way in which its erotic rootage can be the source of generous feelings that produce self-giving love. From this point it can either, at worst, degenerate into a selfishly lustful concern for one's own erotic satisfaction or, at best, advance to find its fulfilment in a unified devotion of the whole self, the feelings accepting the discipline of a mind-controlled will.

There are dangers involved in movement in either direction. Those besetting degeneration need no elaboration. They have been the common stock of moralists' warnings and preachers' denunciations for many a long day. To these I will only add that in my own experience on more than one occasion I have felt that the fact of physical infidelity was not so shocking as its evidence of callous cruelty, the readiness of a husband to leave the wife who for many years has loved and cared for him and borne him children because she can no longer compete with the attraction of a younger woman who reminds him of what she had been when first they were engaged and married. We hear less of the dangers besetting the way of advance. But they are no less formidable. To the selfish cruelty of lustful men there can correspond an equally selfish lack of charity, of understanding sympathy, among the continent. Is Miss Furlong's impression that 'the trouble with the Christians is . . . that they don't seem to care very much' due to there being too much of this about? Do we need to lay more stress on the truth that this is one of the 'corrupt affections' which on Easter Eve we pray for grace to mortify?

Those to whom we are to try to minister will be somewhere on this journey. The question is whether, from our point of view, they are going to go forward or backward and how best we can help them to go forward.

We should now be able to talk sensibly with those who

want help in discriminating between what is morally better and what worse outside as well as inside marriage. The criterion I have just mentioned, the question whether a sexual partnership is tending towards fulfilment or degeneration, is of equal importance in either case. Its moral quality is derived from what is being made of it in itself rather than from its legal or ecclesiastical status. This is not to underrate the moral value of the act whereby men and women undertake the social responsibility of the marriage bond, or the way in which that bond can itself contribute to the enrichment and fulfilment of the love. But the question I have now raised is the one that must surely be the fundamental one in all our thought about sex ethics. Care for it will go a long way towards making marriages more socially valuable and happier. It will also help the unmarried to make the most fruitful use of their lives.

Some of these will be among those to whom I have referred as agreeing with some or all of what I have said under my seven headings a few pages back. It will help them to realize that, as their whole lives are to be dedicated to the service of God and lived to his honour, so by his grace they can conserve their sexual energy for its possible future use in marriage and meanwhile be the more vigorous and sympathetically understanding in other relationships and useful activities. But many will not see things like this. They will see neither rhyme nor reason in the convention that sexual intercourse should be limited to those who are united in lifelong monogamy. Many, indeed, will believe that without experience of such intercourse men and women are deprived of an ingredient essential to any life that is truly worth living.

In each case we have to try to meet people *where they are*, asking how best they can be helped to move forward *from there*. Here comes in the importance of the second and third of my seven headings. So long as we are thinking of God as concerned to select a certain number of men and women for eternal bliss, and of the church as the company of those who are being rescued for their own salvation, our thought of church discipline will be based on attempts to determine the rules which must be kept by those who would be church members in good standing. Moreover, if we think of lifelong monogamy as the universal rule for all Christians in all times and all places, laid down once for all by Christ in the New Testament, we shall tend to regard conformity to this rule as a requirement for communicant membership.

But if we think of the church as the company of those enlisted to carry on Christ's work for the welfare of our heavenly Father's world, the case is altered. Still more so when we take into account what we are learning about the historical origin of Christianity, the meaning of the doctrine of the incarnation, and the relation of the biblical evidence to the general study of human sexuality. We think of the church as entrusted with a gospel that includes the good news, that in human life sex can be enabled to make its best and fullest contribution to good living through faithfulness in monogamous marriage.

The world of nineteen hundred years ago could not be expected to grasp an idea so novel and incredible. It was an idea which required for its actualization the basing of marriage on a Christlike quality of love in an equality of partnership between men and women. Moreover it demanded a high degree of self-discipline and self-control. The Christian church is still engaged in the task of showing in its own life that by God's grace the thing can be done and is worth doing.

Nineteen hundred years is a very small drop in the ocean of the history of human society. We cannot be surprised that the Christian idea has not won more general acceptance in the world of today. The surprising thing is that it has been successful enough to produce in many minds this unjustified surprise, and in the minds of many Christians the belief that strict conformity to its standards should be expected of all who desire to be members of the church in good standing.

But this, surely, is to slip back into thinking of church membership as involving conformity to rules required to qualify for salvation. Must the same demand be made of all who believe in Jesus Christ as the revelation of God, who seek to respond to his call to work with him for the welfare of his creation, and who need the help they can receive from him through fellowship with other believers in the sacrament of Holy Communion? Must we not believe that he who bids us meet them where they are and help them to go forward from there is ready and willing to do the same himself? Even when they are at the stage where they can see neither rhyme nor reason in the convention that sexual intercourse should be limited to those united in lifelong monogamy?

If the church is not to insist on this rule as a qualification for communicant membership, how can it be true to its calling to stand for this principle as the fulfilment of God's will for man's sexual life?

We are thinking of the church as enlisted to be the body through which the risen Lord is carrying on his work of winning back the world to conformity with the Father's will. Within this body some are called and appointed to special offices. St Paul in I Cor. 12 speaks of 'apostles, prophets, teachers, miracle-workers, etc.' Today in the Church of England we have bishops, priests, deacons, lay readers, churchwardens, and other church workers. There are also the members of religious orders, bound by their vows of poverty, chastity and obedience. Too often it has been supposed that those who receive and respond to these special vocations should be regarded as living morally on a higher plane than other Christians. That any such claim should be made on their behalf has always been denied by moral theologians. The tendency to make it is a temptation to be resisted. We must not forget that when St Paul wrote I Corinthians there was no break between what we call chapters twelve and thirteen. Those who hold office serve the church by performing functions which shall help the church to serve the world. Unless the service of both ministers and congregations is the expression of genuine love it sounds in God's ears like sounding brass or tinkling cymbals.

According to the New Testament those who were to hold office in the church were required to be monogamous. It seems to me that the church today would be right to exercise the same discipline. We have accepted office in a body which stands for the belief that this is the way of regulating sexual activity in which it can make its best contribution to good human living, and that by the grace of God it can be done. Our task is to commend this belief to the world of our own time and seek to win its acceptance. We cannot do this if we are not prepared to try to live by it ourselves. It is not a call to live on a higher moral plane than our fellow men and women. In all professions there are some specific disciplines which have to be accepted by their practitioners for the effective discharge of their functions. This is one of ours. So much for that.

When we try to commend our beliefs to others it is surely to the positive values rather than to the restrictive practices that attention should be drawn. We can expect a ready hearing when we speak of the ambivalent potentiality of sexual attraction, of its being the source of so much that is best in human life as well as of so much that is worst, a readiness to talk about how the worst may be avoided and the best achieved. We shall perhaps be surprised to find how many of those who have no patience with what they take to be the church's traditional restrictions have nevertheless a quite definite discipline of their own. Repudiating promiscuity they will value sexual intercourse for its enrichment of friendships that involve far more of the personality than the physical attraction, and for this reason will be selective in their choice of the partners with whom they allow themselves to enjoy it. Moreover they will be ready to accept responsibility for the social consequences of what they do, not only for the possible conception of children but also for its influence on the general level of sexual morality in the sections in which they move.

Our aim will be to help them to discover for themselves how all that is best in their sexual experience will draw them on to seek for some more stable and enduring relationship in what has been called monogamous concubinage, if not in actual marriage.

'To discover for themselves.' But all human discovery of truth is our laying hold on what God is revealing to us. All that has been best in their human friendships has been a partial apprehension of a Christlike quality of love. Their first need is to learn that this has come to them from God, that it is his wish that they should enjoy it and develop it in the way that will enable it to give of its best. If we can help them to see it like this, to want to thank God for it, to ask for his continued blessing upon it, and for guidance and strength in their fostering of it, that may be, to begin with, as far as we should expect to get. For just as all our discovery of truth is our receiving of what God reveals, so, too, our discovering is due to the work of the Holy Spirit opening the eyes of our minds to receive. We must not forget that he is at work in others as well as in ourselves, that our vocation to the cure of souls is not a call to do his work for him but, if I may so put it, to try to open doors for him to enter in and do it himself. If their love is to grow into a stable and enduring relationship and eventually, as we hope and pray, into loyal acceptance of the discipline of Christian marriage, it will be by his leading. If on the way he inspires them to seek the help of the Lord in the sacrament of Holy Communion, it will not be for us to say him nay.

IV

There was a story current in Oxford in the days when what is now called Moral Rearmament was trying to make itself known as the Oxford Group Movement. One of its emissaries was said to have got into conversation with a leading rugger or rowing blue (I forget which). In the course of it he alleged that his arguments were all a smoke screen to cover his moral defects. 'Tell me,' he asked, 'aren't you troubled by impure thoughts?' The man thought for a moment and then said, 'No'. 'Do you mean to tell me, in absolute honesty, that you are not troubled by impure thoughts?' 'Yes,' he replied ruminatively, 'Yes, I do. Not troubled a bit. I rather like 'em.'

This anecdote will serve to introduce one further question which I must open up before I close. Was the man's liking 'em a temptation to be resisted, and enjoyment of it a sin to be confessed? Or would that have been to throw back in God's face a gift which his Creator had given him to be enjoyed? This question goes to the heart of the perplexities which beset the Christian mind as we seek to adjust our thought to the circumstances of the present day. We may approach it by considering the subject of masturbation. In my youth this was commonly referred to in religious circles as self-abuse or onanism. It was taken for granted that it was a sin to be confessed by penitents. Moreover religious teachers sought to reinforce resistance to a practice, assumed to be 'wrong in itself' because 'unnatural', by claiming medical support for holding that it would produce physical or psychological disaster. I can well remember the surprise, if not shock, with which early in the nineteen-twenties, in a book written by a responsible exponent of Christian teaching, I came across the statement that when a man gets married he must be prepared to vary his accustomed rhythm of masturbation and agree with his bride on what will suit her as well as him.[16] That was an early date for masturbation to have been recognized as natural rather than unnatural, as consistent with Christian living, as one of those things for which we have to discrimin-

---

[16] My recollection is that this was in a book by T. W. Pym, sometime Canon Missioner in Southwark Cathedral, but I have not been able to verify this reference.

ate between a right and a wrong use instead of condemning it unequivocally as self-abuse.

From this it is an easy transition to the athlete's impure thoughts. I can remember more than one confessor telling me in my youth that for masturbation to be conquered it must be tackled in the sphere of the mind, that an act of bodily self-abuse in the night might be the inevitable outcome of imaginative indulgence on the previous day and therefore no *fresh* sin. This was common stock of confessorial technique. I have used it myself as a would-be orthodox practitioner. And in my early married life I was told by one priest, a man of much repute as a confessor and afterwards an honoured bishop, that whilst at the time I might enjoy having intercourse with my wife, I must not allow myself any anticipatory imaginative enjoyment of it.

I do not think that today any responsible moral theologian would claim medical support for the view that either masturbation or the enjoyment of sexual fantasies are in themselves unnatural vices which bring physical or psychological disaster in their train. The question now before us is that of the direction and the extent in which we need to revise the kind of moral guidance which I received from my Christian teachers in my youth. We have come to see how God continues to reveal his mind and will to us through such channels as the researches of scientists and philosophers. In this way we have received a fuller understanding of his way of working in creation. We have also come to see how the influence of the life and teaching of Jesus Christ has had to make its way in the minds of his followers among all their existing inherited ideas, confirming some and uprooting others, a process which has been going on ever since his coming and is not yet complete. Among the existing inherited ideas with which the Christian church started on its way were sex tabus springing from terror of hostile demonic powers or from fear of incurring moral or ritual defilement, all assuming that women exist for the comfort and convenience of dominant males. Has the time now come when God is calling on us to learn from the researches of doctors, psychologists and sociologists that he wills us to cast out of our sex ethics the remains of a pagan tradition too long preserved in Christian moral theology by a celibate male priesthood? And if we are learning to do this in respect of masturbation and sexual fantasy, shall we have to go further and explore the possibility of there being in God's eyes distinctions of better and worse in extra-marital sexual intercourse, both heterosexual and homosexual? Is the traditional undiscriminating ban indisputably a product of direct divine inspiration? Or is it due in part to these tabus, and, for want of adequate contraceptive techniques, maintained to avoid the kind of social confusion that marriage was devised to prevent?

I have said enough, I hope, to make clear why I think that any discussion of Christian sex ethics today must take the form of an enquiry rather than an exposition. So far as I am concerned it is an open-ended enquiry. I have got as far as I can at my age, and must leave it to younger generations to follow whither God's continuing revelation shall lead them. I have tried throughout my life to live by what I have understood the Christian sex ethic to be, but I could not now say what it is with the same confidence with which I could have asserted it fifty years ago. Month by month, as the twenty-fifth morning brings round the thirty-fourth verse of Psalm 119, I find myself echoing its words with heart-felt devotion, and with appreciation of what both the Hebrew and the English contribute to the meaning of the word 'heart': 'Give me understanding and I shall keep thy law: yea I shall keep it with my whole heart.'

INDEX